Author ph:

Bernadette Russell is an expert on kindness and hope, as well as an author, playwright, storyteller and activist. She is the author of *How to be Hopeful*, *The Little Book of Kindness* and *The Little Book of Wonder*. For over a decade she has toured the US and UK speaking about the life-changing experience of practising kindness, including at the Southbank Centre, where she was nominated as one of sixty-seven change makers for her project 366 Days of Kindness. She has created shows and participatory workshops around the topic for many organizations including the Royal Festival Hall, the Royal Albert Hall, Royal National Theatre, as well as pubs, community centres & libraries around the UK.

**UNCORRECTED PROOF
NOT FOR SALE OR DISTRIBUTION**

Conversations *on* Kindness

How the power of kindness can change the world

BERNADETTE RUSSELL

Elliott&Thompson

First published 2025 by
Elliott and Thompson Limited
2 John Street
London WC1N 2ES
www.eandtbooks.com

ISBN: 978-1-78396-851-0

Copyright © Bernadette Russell 2025

The Author has asserted her rights under the Copyright, Designs and Patents Act, 1988, to be identified as Author of this Work.

All rights reserved. No part of this publication may be reproduced, stored in or introduced into a retrieval system, or transmitted, in any form, or by any means (electronic, mechanical, photocopying, recording or otherwise) without the prior written permission of the publisher. Any person who does any unauthorized act in relation to this publication may be liable to criminal prosecution and civil claims for damages.

9 8 7 6 5 4 3 2 1

A catalogue record for this book is available from the British Library.

Typesetting: Marie Doherty
Printed by Pixel Colour Imaging Ltd, 10 Prestons Road, London E14 9RL

Dedicated to my mum, to my sisters Natalie Russell and Kimberley Trim, to my partner Gareth Brierley and to Lola the Woof.

To all survivors, artists and dreamers everywhere.

And to all of those in the past, present and future who are in service to kindness, many of whom do not receive awards, accolades or recognition, yet who make the world a better place by quietly doing their thing. To them, my love and gratitude, always. I see you and I will do my best to amplify your names and work as often as I can.

Contents

BEFORE
London's Burning   1

1. AUGUST
Try a Little Kindness   17

2. SEPTEMBER
Flower Power   31

3. OCTOBER
Be Kind to All Kinds   43

4. NOVEMBER
Another Day in Paradise   59

5. DECEMBER
I Gotta Have Faith   75

6. JANUARY
The Bad News Blues   87

7. FEBRUARY
What's Love Got to Do With It?   99

8. MARCH
People Ain't No Good   113

9. APRIL
Born to Run   125

10. MAY
Compliment Slips   137

11. JUNE
Amazing Grace   151

12. JULY
Journey's End   163

AFTER
Starfish   177

Chapter Notes   195
Further Reading   201
Who's Who   203
Thanks   211

Before
London's Burning

Stories are compasses and architecture, we navigate by them, we build our sanctuaries and our prisons out of them, and to be without a story is to be lost in the vastness of a world that spreads in all directions like arctic tundra or sea ice.

Rebecca Solnit, *The Faraway Nearby*

Hello, and thank you in advance for reading this book. Just so you know what you are getting yourself into, it's about the experiment I began back on 18 August 2011, when I tried to do a kind thing for a stranger every single day for a year and a day, to see if kindness could change the world. And it's about the decade since, as I have continued my daily practice of kindness, deepening my understanding of its power and potential for positive change in the wider world, in my community and in my life. Since that transformative day, I've written and performed a theatre show about my experiences which has toured the UK for over ten years. I have made dozens of community art projects with kindness at their heart, with many organisations including the Royal Albert Hall and the Royal Festival Hall. I've written five books about kindness, hope and community for adults and children, as well as dozens of articles on the subject for newspapers, websites and magazines. I have been one of the subjects of a BBC1 television documentary about kindness, as well as featuring in a PRX radio documentary about kindness in the USA. I have spoken about kindness on many podcasts and radio shows. But most significantly, I have changed the way I work, live and think, by intentionally aiming to place kindness at the centre of everything I do and every decision I make.

The story I'm about to tell you, about that first year and what happened afterwards, is a pretty messy one. Some of it is sad. Some of it is joyful. Bits are funny, silly, surprisingly, unlikely and infuriating. Some parts might irritate you. Sometimes the protagonist (me) is annoying and makes bad choices. The story zips about in time a bit, and in it I have conversations with many wonderful people for whom kindness is at the centre of their work and lives: scientists, artists, activists and academics who have helped me dive deeper into what kindness is and what it is capable of; who have helped me answer the question, 'Can kindness change the world?'

Before you read on, let me tell you: this journey changed my life and I think it has the potential to change yours. I know this is a bold statement, and I make it quite deliberately: I think certain stories do have the power to transform lives.

This is a story about kindness, but it is also a story about resilience and hope. I'm sharing it as a reminder to myself, and to you, that the world is fuelled by love. That we already have everything we need to make the world a better place. It's an audacious thing to say in the present circumstances, I know. I ask you to stay with me.

> If you are despairing . . .
> If you feel lost . . .
> If you feel powerless . . .
> If you are overwhelmed . . .
> If you want to do something but don't know what to do . . .
> If you are tired of hurting . . .
> If you are tired of worrying . . .
> If you are tired of being sad . . .

London's Burning

If you are longing for something better . . .

If you're sick of the bad news . . .

If you sometimes secretly fear you just don't like human beings much any more . . .

. . . then this book is for you. And if you are none of those things, but you are curious, or you just like a good story, well then, this book is for you too.

Some of it is full of light and beauty, and some of it is dark, and most of it sits in the messy middle, just like life.

It starts in the dark, back in the 1970s when I was a little kid. Way back to when it all began for me. A trigger warning: without gratuitous detail I am going to talk now about my very difficult childhood. If you'd rather skip this part, I get it, you can go to page 7 and just know I was motivated by my childhood experiences to prove to myself that there was good in the world. If you're okay with reading on, here goes . . .

When I was a very small child, I found out suddenly that some grown-ups could be cruel and were not to be trusted.

I was three when my mum and dad split up. My dad was in the army and he stayed on his base in Germany; my mum took me and my sister Natalie back to live with her parents in Leicester. My dad didn't want to see us any more, although we didn't know why. I didn't see him again for over forty years.

My mum was very young and very pretty and felt trapped and frustrated staying with our grandparents, even though she loved them a lot. They were old-fashioned and protective, and treated her a bit like a child. Natalie and I, on the other hand, loved living with them and loved their house. We loved Leicester and the sari shops filled with jewel-coloured dresses and rows of sparkling bangles. How everyone said 'me duck'.

Mum got a job in a pub and tried to rent a flat, but the prospective landlady wouldn't rent it to her as she was worried about two little girls and their mum living on their own. I But it was really hard for my mum.

Conversations on Kindness

She craved independence and a new start. When I was four and my sister two, Mum married a man who had a good job and who could give us all a home and provide for us.

Unbeknown to Mum, though, our stepdad was an abuser: sadistic, cruel and an expert manipulator. He made sure she never had the faintest idea of what he was up to. The man who had replaced our absent father treated me and my sister as if we were worthless. It's well documented that predators are expert at concealing their actions and intentions, and I want to be clear that I do not hold my mum in any way responsible for what happened to us as children. In a very real way, it happened to her too – she is also a survivor of his abuses.

So, my lovely mum had married a man we were terrified of and whom we both feared and pitied. While he lived with us, my sister and I never told each other what was happening because we didn't have the words to explain it. We each thought and hoped it was only happening to us.

Our stepdad kept changing jobs, after being asked to leave for reasons that remain unclear. We moved so often we never put down roots or felt we really belonged anywhere. We were always the new ones at school. We were both extremely shy and didn't know what to say to other kids (but we had each other). We had things to hide. We were ashamed. We escaped reality through stories and books, we played long, complicated games in which we cast ourselves as heroines who escaped evil and poverty to become rich and happy.

In real life we weren't well off. We had that humiliation common to so many people without much money, of having unfashionable and scruffy clothes, and being conscious that money was tight and that we should not always expect to get the things we wanted. I was always scared, often sad and sometimes outright terrified. I covered my walls in pictures of animals, which I loved fiercely and felt a profound connection with. My sister got into stargazing and escaped that way. We each tried in our

London's Burning

own ways to draw attention to our unhappiness, but it was not picked up on and help didn't arrive.

Eventually we settled in rural Hampshire, the place I still think of as home.

My grandparents provided light in this darkness when we stayed with them in the summer holidays. We four sat at their dining-room table in Leicester and made up poems. Grandad would walk us up the garden and show us his flowers and vegetables. Nana wrote us poems and took us swimming. They made us fat chips fried in lard with eggs for tea and bacon sandwiches for breakfast; they played Jim Reeves records and sang along to Grandmaster Flash on Radio One. I think my nana was the first elderly white lady to know all the lyrics to Sugarhill Gang's 'Rapper's Delight'. Grandad told the same jokes over and over again – 'Last night I dreamed I was eating shredded wheat and when I woke up half the mattress was gone' – and we laughed every time he told them. They had a sideboard filled with sweets and broken biscuits from Leicester market and we'd sit and watch *Top of the Pops* on the TV and eat all the sweets and Grandad would say it was 'like a dog had been at them'. He sang 'You Are My Sunshine' and 'I Did It My Way' to my nana every night.

They gave us unconditional love. My grandparents taught me and my sister what kindness is and how to relax and enjoy yourself when you aren't under threat all the time. We were so happy there. Our lovely Mum taught us by example how to be kind to people, so despite our stepdad's shadowy presence, we did have adults we could depend upon for love and guidance.

Eventually, when I was thirteen, my stepdad left. Once he was gone my sister and I shared our experiences with each other and plucked up the courage to tell our mum. We had a little sister now, his daughter, and we didn't want the same to happen to her – at eleven and thirteen we felt big enough to protect her. Mum listened, devastated, believed us without hesitation and called the police right away. The police came and interviewed us. We didn't understand their questions. They phoned Mum soon afterwards to tell her that there wasn't enough evidence to prosecute him. Our extended family did not want to talk about it – I think they may have been ashamed. Some family members told us that they had felt something was wrong with our stepdad, which was why they kept their kids away from him all these years. Other adults who might have helped – teachers, friends and professionals – failed our little family in their various ways. My mum was left to cope with the terrible aftermath of our revelation with very little support.

At some point we were visited by a social worker. I believe she was trying to comfort us when she said, 'Don't worry, unfortunately there are lots of people like him in the world, in lots of other houses.' My sister and I were both horrified. We would much rather have heard that he was the only one she had ever heard of, because that would have meant we were safe now we were away from him. But apparently not so. It seemed the world was populated by monsters. How the hell could we survive in a world full of houses occupied by people like him? Why were there so many? Why were they allowed to be like that, when we had to quietly get on with our lives with no help?

I was so bloody angry.

Also, I just would not believe it, I would not accept it. It didn't make sense. Everyone, even him, had to have some light in them, didn't they? And there were loads more good people than bad, weren't there? After all, there was only one of him in my life, and I also had my mum, my sisters, my grandparents, my friends.

I think that moment was when it began really – my mission to prove to myself and to everyone around me that the world was a good place and the people in it were good too. This need to prove a point was seeded by fear.

I started with myself. I tried to be as nice as I possibly could be. Obviously I can sometimes be as grumpy, mean and selfish as the next

London's Burning

person, but for the most part I worked very hard at being kind. People at college would say, 'You're too nice' and my English teacher said I was 'generous to a fault'. I gave away clothes, money, ideas, food – it was as though I was throwing things into the abyss because of my fear that under the surface was a deep well of darkness.

I constructed a way of being in the world that made me feel safe, but it wasn't very robust because I didn't really have a guiding principle. I was busy putting on lipstick and drinking snakebite and black, and listening to goth bands in nightclubs in Portsmouth, so it took me a while to find my compass. For a long time I was a mixture of genuinely heartfelt trying-to-be-a-good-person intentions and a little ball of rage and fear. To be honest, probably a typical teenager. To be fair, a pretty average human being.

As I travelled through life, I realised how much suffering there was, all around me, and how much I had to be grateful for. There is always someone worse off than you, and the realisation of how fortunate I am has grown as I get older. But still, I carried this wound.

Eventually I went to university, then to drama school. I abandoned my original ambition of being a vet in favour of being an actor. I wanted to be famous. Deep down I hoped that if I was famous my dad might see me on TV and reach out. Maybe even my stepdad would be full of remorse and ask my forgiveness. I didn't have that kind of self-awareness then. I always told people, and myself, that I had chosen acting because it would give me an exciting life – simple as that.

I managed to just about scrape a living doing small-scale tours of theatre shows around the UK. Like many people who choose the theatre as a profession, I often suffered existential angst – a pretty expression for sweaty, insomnia-inducing horror. *No, no, no, I've made an awful mistake, I think I've ruined my whole stupid pointless life! Why didn't I stick it out at Barrett's shoes while I had the chance? They offered me management training!* These thoughts have been induced on tour; by near bankruptcy;

by occasional experiences of mild carbon-monoxide poisoning suffered while sitting in a lay-by on the M4, observing someone else trying to fix a broken-down white van whose back was filled with spine-destroying sets which we often had to carry up three flights of narrow stairs as the venue's lifts were broken or never existed; and idle afternoons spent wandering around identikit shopping centres that smelled of pine disinfectant and mild disappointment.

'This is where my dreams have led me,' I could be heard muttering to myself, staring wanly out of a rain-splattered window at another anonymous stretch of motorway.

There wasn't an awful lot in the way of validation. The wound I was carrying wasn't healed by choosing this life, but I was pleasantly distracted. In the background always was this nagging feeling that there was something I meant to do that I hadn't done yet. That I wasn't going to find what I was looking for here.

But there were loads of compensations: I have often laughed so hard during work that I have fallen over, made lifelong friends with some wonderful, interesting, hilarious, eccentric people. I have seen parts of the UK I would undoubtably never have got round to visiting; been all around the world; I've done shows in theatres of all sizes, as well as in phone boxes and on boats and in old factories; I've had standing ovations and received awards and looked out on banks of seats filled with people laughing and crying or just watching, rapt. I've extended the time that you are usually allowed to wear fancy dress/pretend you're an animal/put on silly accents merely by virtue of calling myself an actor. I have used a *lot* of glitter.

In those early post-drama school years, I was still trying to be a good person. I recycled, I voted, I signed petitions. I was a vegetarian. I tried to be nice, polite, punctual, put my loose change in the charity buckets at the tube station.

I had watched the news less and less; when I did, it was through meshed fingers. I felt overwhelmed, even back then. It was so depressing.

London's Burning

This feeling of helplessness I could track back to the march against the war in Iraq on 15 February 2003 that *everyone* was on: Home Counties mums, inner-city college kids, crusties, passionate lefties, religious folk of all kinds, everyone. It felt incredibly powerful and important and life-changing. Until nothing changed. The war carried on. Tony Blair disgraced himself, the news of weapons of mass destruction was a load of bollocks, and everybody said how many of us would it take to march until something changed? It didn't feel like democracy, the reaction to that march. It felt like someone saying, 'Shut up, fools. Be quiet.'

After that it was harder for me to work up enthusiasm for being politically active even in a small way. This wasn't a conscious decision, I just let it fade away. I wandered around Topshop in Oxford Street and forgot to buy fair-trade coffee. I had a purse full of maxed-out credit cards and I found it hard to be optimistic.

Still, when I went to the Edinburgh Festival in 2011 I was happy. Sort of.

'Happy on top,' as my ex-flatmate Amanda Cuellar used to say, seeing straight through my brittle grin. 'But sad under.'

Underneath the fizzy adrenaline of enjoying what at best felt like a paid holiday, maybe I was a little bit down. I was sad because of all the horror of the news. I was sad because of neglected dogs left to pine in empty flats, and the old lady dead for three days before anyone noticed, and the boy who committed suicide because he got bullied on Facebook, and because of benefit cuts to people who needed them most, and Tesco's selling padded bras for eight-year-old girls, and children's science toys only stocked in the boys' section, and the woman who got arrested and threatened with stoning for falling in love, and bombs ending the lives of children playing on beaches, and girls hurt in the name of tradition, and endless bloody wars which no one seemed to have the power or the courage to stop, and refugee camps as big as countries, and people burning down forests and mosques and synagogues and churches, and rising sea levels and species extinctions and cruelty to animals and oil shortages and crop failures and global warming and bloody twerking. And I was sad because I was still carrying an old wound that had never healed.

I didn't notice it consciously, this undercurrent of sadness. It was like the magma that Mr McFadden taught us about in geography lessons, underneath Earth's crust. I carried on oblivious on the surface of it, knowing it was there but not paying it any attention.

I was at the aforementioned Edinburgh Festival with Penny Dreadful Theatre Company. It was the morning after the first night of our show, and I was sitting with my friends reviving myself with a fry-up at my favourite café, The City Café, when on the TV I saw some terrible sights. A twenty-nine-year-old black man called Mark Duggan had been shot and killed by police in Tottenham, North London. A gathering of about forty people, including the mother of Mark Duggan's children, Semone Wilson, gathered at the police station to ask questions, only to be turned away. There had been no official confirmation of his death at that point, so his family and friends found out via what they saw and heard in the media. The negative impact and frustration that built in the days that followed led to the unrest that is usually described as a riot. However, many community leaders and frontline workers saw it as a protest born out of a widespread sense of social injustice.

Soon the unrest spread from London to Manchester, Birmingham, Bristol and beyond. Back in Edinburgh, on the TV screen in front of me, I saw double-decker buses on fire, shops burned to the ground, businesses looted. It looked like civil war had broken out. Like there'd been this boiling rage just underneath the surface that suddenly exploded. On the news they said there'd not been that many in fires in London since the Blitz. People were scared, or angry, or both. There were calls to bring in the army, or water cannons, to deal with the rioters.

This was the last straw for me. There was something about this expression of rage and grief that brought all the bad news to the surface.

London's Burning

It wasn't simply the unrest and fires and looting, although that was bad enough, but also the reaction from the press – no one seemed to care about finding out why they had happened, they just dished out blame. Tabloids called the riots the 'Chav Spring', Richard Littlejohn wrote in the *Daily Mail* that the rioters 'should be clubbed like baby seals' and David Starkey said the riots happened because 'the whites have become black'. It was all so racist, classist and depressing.

Even in Edinburgh, in that magical month when the festival is on and the 'real world' seems so far away, the riots stayed in our minds and conversations.

Blame was piled on what some in the media decided were the 'usual suspects' (black people, brown people, poor people, young people), but we soon found out that in fact all kinds of people had grabbed a free pair of trainers from the kicked-in windows of Foot Locker. I wasn't the only one who remembered the words of Martin Luther King Junior who cautioned, 'A riot is the language of the unheard.' It didn't seem like anyone in power was even attempting to listen to those unheard voices.

A week after the riots had started, I came back home from Edinburgh to Deptford, South East London. Back to reality. The whole of the capital seemed unusually quiet and subdued. I felt useless, thinking about it all, powerless to make any kind of meaningful, positive contribution to anything. What was I doing with my one 'wild and precious life' when there was so much urgent trouble?

But I did notice little shoots of hope.

On the front pages of newspapers, images of buses on fire were replaced by pictures of groups of people with brooms held aloft, people who'd joined in #riotcleanup, a campaign started by poet and artist Dan Thompson on Twitter, as a practical response to the riots. He started tweeting around midnight on the Monday after the unrest had started, encouraging people to 'start with the smallest thing possible . . . get a broom, get a bin bag and start clearing up your local shop' — and by midday on Tuesday he had 76,000 followers.

In one of the places badly hit by the riots, Rye Lane, around the corner from where I live, someone stuck up a Post-it note which said, 'We all love Peckham! Peace.' It was soon joined by hundreds more tiny squares of messages of love and respect for the local community and came to be known as the Peckham Peace Wall. Walking past it, you could see it put a smile back on the faces of passers-by, and it was easy for people to contribute to.

These stories of people looking out for each other and their communities gave me courage, and just a little bit of hope. I felt sure there was something I could do to contribute meaningfully. I just didn't know what yet.

Then on 18 August 2011, a perfectly ordinary day, I was in a queue at the Post Office in Deptford. There was a young man in front of me. I vaguely noticed his hoodie, his downcast eyes, his scuffed trainers. I remember thinking, *I bet you are having a hard time right now. You look like all those images of rioters we have been presented with on TV.* I felt for him. I thought about assumptions that might be made about him. How he had been affected by recent events, too. I overheard him talking to the man behind the counter; he said sorry that he didn't have enough money for his stamp, that it was more than he had expected it to be. As he walked away, I said, 'I'll pay for it.'

He seemed completely taken aback by that tiny act of kindness. It was nothing much, a little bit of money and time, but he said thanks several times and we smiled at each other. It felt good to do. I thought to myself: *Well, that was easy. Making him smile was easy. Maybe, that 50p and a few moments of my time did make a small difference to him in that moment...*

I got on the bus, thinking about what had just happened, the effect it might have had on the young man, and on me, and on the people in the Post Office who saw it. It was such a small act but it seemed pretty powerful, like the Post-its on the Peckham Peace Wall.

By the time I got home, I knew exactly what I wanted to do. Even thinking it gave me a big rush of adrenaline. I was going to try to do a kind thing for a stranger every single day for a year. For 366 days, I realised, because it would cover a leap year. I was going to see if kindness could change the world...

Before I continue, I'd like to confess to the not-so-kind things I did before I started. I don't want you to feel you are about to get a saccharine, virtue-signalling festival of vainglory. I was definitely not perfect. I'm still not. Here are some highlights, in date order, of just some of the things that make me feel guilty, or ashamed, or both, and definitely not kind:

- When I was six, I tied my little sister Natalie to a swing at the bottom of our garden with a length of washing line and I left her there for ages while I went in and ate a Findus crispy pancake.

- When I was seven, I threw a brick at my best friend Christopher Walker's head because I wanted to see what brains looked like.

- When I was ten, I forced our cat into a blue baby doll's outfit, which said, 'I am a boy' on the front. Then I put the cat into a pram and pushed it round the neighbourhood all day. And the cat was a girl. Not that cats care about gender conformity, but still...

- When I was eleven, I told my teacher our house had burned to the ground in a terrible accident, just to get out of doing double PE, and I was called into the head teacher's office for counselling.

- When I was twelve, I wrote 'Mary is a silly cow' on the wall of Purbrook Park School and I drew her head onto the body of a cow. It was an excellent drawing of both her and the cow, although I realise this is beside the point.

Conversations on Kindness

- When I was thirteen, I dumped the entire contents of my Saturday morning paper round into an ornamental pond, and I told the newsagents a rival paper girl had attacked me.

- When I was fourteen, I kicked a boy just because he looked like the 1980s pop star Simon Le Bon.

- When I was nineteen, I glued matchsticks to the hairs on my friend Alex's legs with superglue while she was asleep.

- When I was twenty-two, I was sick inside my friend Geraldine Daley's hat, and I never owned up.

- When I was twenty-six, my friend told me about the time she went on holiday to Greece. She was really excited to be on holiday abroad without her parents for the first time. She ate a lot of unfamiliar, very rich food, as you do, and the next morning, on the way back to her caravan from having breakfast, found herself caught short with a gurgling tummy. She had to squat behind a bush and just poo and poo and poo until it all came out. I retold that story to everyone I knew (and I am now writing it down for publication).

- When I was thirty, I pushed a woman into a bin full of garlic on Deptford High Street just because she shouted at me.

- When I was thirty-four, I escaped out of my friend's play by pretending to faint, but the real reason was I was really, really bored.

- When I was thirty-six, I poured very hot Tabasco sauce into my partner Gareth's mouth while he was asleep.

- When I was thirty-eight, I put raw sardines in my friend Ian's shoes at a barbecue and let him put his feet back in the shoes without telling him.

- When I was forty, I was asked to do a short phone survey for Transport for London, but I said it wasn't possible because 'Bernadette Russell is sadly dead'.

- When I was forty-three, I said, 'Don't bitch me, bitch' to a customs officer on the Vienna to Bratislava ferry and to this day I would hesitate to put my foot back in Slovakia.

And there have been a lot more since then. Grumpy mornings, thinking the worst of people, taking more than my fair share of pizza, you know the kind of thing. I hope the list gives you an idea of who you are dealing with.

I do admit that I was (and am still) prone to what my partner Gareth refers to as 'madcap schemes'. I'd previously told him I was going to take my HGV licence because I loved the idea of driving a massive truck, but I hadn't even got my normal licence yet. I once decided I was going to do a diploma course in Ghost Hunting at the Paranormal Academy. That's a real course. And just the week before I had decided I was going to leave showbiz entirely and retrain as a dog whisperer. None of these madcap schemes came to fruition. I get easily excited, you see. Then I run out of steam, just as easily.

But not this time. This time was different. I thought to myself, *Come on, you can do this! You know you have never really been the best at anything, so maybe, just maybe, you could be the best at being kind.* So, I posted my intentions on Facebook and Twitter; they got two likes and twelve comments, which seemed epic at the time and was all the encouragement I needed.

For fun, here's a list of some things that definitely came in handy for me in that first year and a day:

Good walking boots
Water

Conversations on Kindness

A sense of humour

Tissues

Germolene

Plasters

Good listening skills

Good observational skills

Crafting skills (optional)

Glue (optional)

A change of clothes in case you suddenly go to a party

Pen and paper

GPS

The ability to spot people who might be receptive to a conversation with a stranger

Friendly demeanour

Thick skin *and* sensitivity

Readiness to learn some uncomfortable truths about yourself (like you get angry if people don't say thank you)

Readiness to forgive yourself once you've learned the uncomfortable truths, to withstand loneliness, despair, sorrow and exhaustion. But also to enjoy spontaneity, mischief, creativity, conversation, parties, cakes, surprise turns of events, startling revelations, shocking confessions and sudden changes of weather and opinion.

Ready? Let's go . . .

1. AUGUST

Try a Little Kindness

> *Five acts of kindness this month:*
>
> **Day 5:** I hid £5 inside a book in Waterstones, Greenwich, with a note saying, 'Enjoy.'
>
> **Day 7:** I gave a stranger at the bus stop a packet of love hearts.
>
> **Day 9:** I left a packet of Liquorice Allsorts in a phone box in Shoreditch with a note saying 'Eat me.'
>
> **Day 10:** I chalked the Wendell Berry poem 'The Peace of Wild Things' on to the pathway of our local park, in the hope it might make people smile.
>
> **Day 14:** I gave a stranger an 'unbirthday present' – beautifully wrapped and containing chocolate, hand cream, sweets and a mini sparkler.

Well, I'd had the call to adventure, even though you could say I'd called myself. And I was very eager to set out.

I was freelancing as a picture researcher three days a week. It was a very busy and stressful job. The rest of the week I worked on my monthly storytelling show at an arts centre in East London. I had very little disposable income. So, time *and* cash poor. But also, fairly secure with work, which was unusual for me, and with a public platform via my storytelling show. Plus I worked with very supportive and interested people who got involved with my mission from the start. So I had a lot on my side.

My incredibly supportive partner, Gareth, was in the midst of training for the London Marathon, so he had some good ideas about how you can support yourself when setting out on a big challenge. He suggested that I might like to write some rules. It might be fun and put some boundaries around the whole idea.

Here they are.

The Rules of Kindness

1. Thou[1] must be kind to a stranger every single day for a year. Basic requirement.
2. Thou must never say no if someone asks thou for money (yes, I know, foolish, and yes, it got expensive).
3. Every single day thou must smile at a stranger and not sulk if they don't smile back.
4. Thou can sponsor people, but this is very easy, so thou can only do it if thou are ill or somehow incapacitated.
5. It must be a wide variety of people, not just people thou like the look of. In fact, it should especially be people thou don't like the look of.
6. It doesn't count if it's just normal everyday politeness, like saying thank you. It should be an *uncommon act of kindness*.
7. Thou must record it every day on Facebook and Twitter.
8. Other people can join in, but thou can't make them.
9. No days off. No exceptions – however ill, hungover or maimed,[2] thou must do it . . . *whatever happens*.
10. It must be a different thing every day.[3]

---

[1] I addressed myself as thou, in my journal, to be playful, and to make it seem more like a commandment.

[2] I actually wrote 'maimed'. I don't know what I thought was going to happen to me!

[3] This last 'commandment' was broken almost immediately, as some things worked so well and were so much fun that they were worth repeating. And besides, 366 different ideas is a *lot*.

Try a Little Kindness

So I had my rules sorted. I'd posted the idea on social media. I was ready. But first I had to work out how to approach people. What should I say to start the conversation? I didn't want to scare anyone. I didn't want them to think that I was trying to sell them something or that I was asking for donations – so I realised that I needed to be friendly, but not over friendly, and I needed to be able to explain quickly and clearly what my intentions were.

I also realised I had to consider who to approach. Should I go for the easy route, and choose someone who looked familiar and friendly? Approaching that kind of person would be the path of least resistance. But I had promised to approach 'a wide variety of people', so should I take the opportunity to really stretch myself and go for someone who looked angry, or unfriendly, or intimidating? And what would make me decide that someone might be unfriendly or intimidating? I decided to pay attention to my conscious and unconscious biases as I went on, and to challenge myself on them when they presented themselves.

On Day Two, I went out into the world to try it. Specifically, I went into the Tesco's near where I live. (It occurs to me that this might be the only time in history that a great adventure has been recorded as beginning in a British supermarket.) I'd already decided that I was going to buy some flowers and give them to somebody. *Everyone likes flowers*, I thought. I chose some and went to the checkout to pay. As I approached, I saw Ryan on the checkout. I knew his name was Ryan because he was wearing one of those little name badges. Adele's 'Someone Like You' was playing quietly in the background, and I thought Ryan looked a bit sad. *Maybe he isn't having a very good day*, I thought. So I decided to give the flowers to Ryan. I was *very* nervous.

This is how our conversation went:

Me: Hello . . . um . . . Ryan. My name's Bernadette. Bernadette Russell. Sorry if this is a bit weird. You know the riots that just happened?

Conversations on Kindness

Ryan: Mmm.

Me: Well, it was horrible, wasn't it?

Ryan: Mmm.

Me: Well, I decided after that . . . I was going to do a kind act for a stranger every day and I brought these flowers and then I saw you . . . and you look nice.

Ryan: Mmm.

Me: So, I wondered if you would accept this and be my today's act of kindness?

PAUSE (*which seemed to last for eternity, but was probably ten seconds max*)

Ryan (*with amazing enthusiasm and incredible volume*): 'OH MY GOD THAT IS BRILLIANT! IT'S SO COOL. THANK YOU SO MUCH!'

I was absolutely delighted. I loved Ryan in that moment. I went out of Tesco's walking on air. 'Bye, Ryan! Thank you, Ryan!' I called as I left.

So that was Day Two. A success.

The next day, Day Three, I was feeling very optimistic after the previous day's triumph. I was on the number 47 bus coming home from Greenwich, and I had prepared a book to give to someone. It was a fantastic book called *When God Was a Rabbit* by Sarah Winman. I had already read it and loved it – plus regifting is environmentally friendly, of course. I wrote inside it, 'Dear Stranger, hope you enjoy this book, love Bernadette xxx.'

I quickly decided to give it to the grumpy-looking man sitting opposite me, even though I was a little nervous of doing so. But I paid attention to the fact that here I was *assuming* he was grumpy rather than knowing for sure, based on my interpretation of his expression. He could just be thinking about annoying things. He could be having a terrible day. Then I started thinking about how *maybe* grumpy-looking people get nice stuff happening to them less often, because people might be put off by the grumpiness of their expressions. I wondered if therefore I should find the grumpiest looking person on the bus and give the book to them. I was overthinking it, and to be honest I was basically spoilt for choice on the bus that afternoon. It was a dull day and who sits on a bus grinning anyway? My stop came, and I got off the bus, but I still had the book in my hand, so I started looking around for a likely target.

O my God, I'm thinking 'target' like a serial killer, I thought, and that made me more nervous, but it also made me laugh a bit. In the end I went up to a friendly looking woman who got off the bus at the same time as me and said, 'Would you please accept this gift of a book as my good deed for the day?'

'Thanks very much, I will,' she said, and put it in her bag for life.

So that was okay. I hope I didn't alarm her. I saw her jump a bit when I first spoke. I hoped I'd get the hang of this soon. Saying 'good deed for the day' was a keeper as a way of putting people at ease – I reckoned pretty much everyone knew what that meant.

Day Four was August Bank Holiday. From the very beginning I had wanted this mission to be creative. I knew straight away that some days the opportunity to be kind would present itself, but I also wanted to be prepared and arty. So I got out my craft kit and spent a long time making a gorgeous card, with sequins, glitter, a bit of collage, illustrations. The works. I really went to town, and I wrote inside:

> Dear Stranger,
> I hope you are enjoying the Bank Holiday. I dare you to call in sick tomorrow and have another day in the sunshine with your friends.
> love from your Fairy Godmother.

I was so excited about this. I kept imagining how thrilled I would be if I received a card like that, from a Fairy Godmother. I thought it would be like living in a real-life Disney movie – amazing.

I got to London Bridge Station. It's a large, very busy concourse with people dashing about as you'd expect, but soon I saw this friendly looking man, so I decided to give my carefully crafted card to him. This is how it went:

Me (*hand outstretched with the card*): Hello. I wanted to give you this.
Him: I don't want it.
Me: Oh! Don't worry, honestly, it's really nice.
Him: I don't want it.
Me: But . . . it took me ages to make it . . . and it's a good thing, I promise you.
Him: I don't want it.
Me (*shouting*): PLEASE PLEASE TAKE IT TAKE IT TAKE IT!

I kind of threw it at his head and ran down the escalator as fast as I could.

Oh no. No. Cringe. What had just occurred wasn't good.

It wasn't really a kindness. I mean, it could be said to be approaching common assault. I decided I couldn't count that one, so I left a pound coin on the tube seat with a little note saying 'Take me' for someone to pick up later.

Perhaps this wasn't going to be as easy I thought. And I still had 362 days to go. Wow.

I had learned an important lesson: that what might be a kindness to me (receiving a mysterious handmade card) is not necessarily a kindness for someone else, especially when they are running for a train. So I shouldn't anticipate their response going a particular way, or at least I should notice when I was anticipating, to protect myself from disappointment. It was complicated. But also, more interesting than I had hoped for, and requiring more courage and determination than I'd expected.

I was nervous and excited at the prospect of continuing, as well as a bit ashamed of throwing a card at a man, and worried that he might have got a paper cut. I berated myself for not having explained to him why I was giving him a card, and began to spiral with worry about the possible paper cut (what if it festers and he gets sepsis?, etc.).

It was at this point that I checked my messages and saw something on Facebook. It was from Ryan in Tesco's: 'I have just been the lucky receiver of a "Random act of kindness"!' it said. 'I was given a beautiful flowering plant, totally out of the blue by a fellow Londoner, happily spreading joy on her way home from work. It has made me feel so wonderful and so special and once again has opened my heart and eyes to how wonderful life is. Thank you, Bernadette, sending love to you this evening and love to everyone else out there ☺ Ryan.'

He might not have realised it, but Ryan's message gave me courage to go on. His reciprocal kindness came at exactly the right moment. It convinced me that yes, I still had a long way to go, but I could do this. He'd remembered my name. He'd found me and thanked me, publicly. It was working. Yes!

Suddenly, I was ready for the next day, and the next encounter with a stranger.

In just four days I had experienced a wide range of responses from strangers (quiet gratitude, enthusiastic joy, friendly bewilderment and refusal to engage) and had experienced a range of emotional responses myself (from mild to wild joy to disappointment to frustrated panic).

Dr Gillian Sandstrom is Senior Lecturer in the Psychology of Kindness at the University of Sussex. The university's Centre for Research on Kindness would, some years later, conduct a wonderful research project called The Kindness Test, which I will delve into more deeply later. Dr Sandstrom's work within that project focused on the importance and significance of talking to strangers, so as I reflected on the beginning of this year of kindness, I was curious about what she had discovered. First of all, I wanted to know about the science behind the benefits of talking with people we don't already know.

The Kindness of Strangers
with Dr Gillian Sandstrom

All your work and research is fascinating, but I'm particularly interested in work you've done around the benefits of talking to strangers and I wondered if you could tell me about that?

Well, there's something especially freeing about talking to strangers. I'm very much an introvert, and I think it works for introverts because I feel like I have full control. I can choose to initiate a conversation with someone. I know it's not going to last, and I'm going to walk away at the end. So it feels low risk and less scary. It just feels safer to me.

Yes, I feel the same! I am also very interested in what you think happens when you just keep on doing something, which I know you've looked at in your studies.

Yeah, there's something in the psychology of habits. That things just get easier if we do them a bunch. I ran a study where I had people talk to a stranger every day for a week. They would say it went better than they expected, and none of the things they worried about actually happened. But people need to see that there's a pattern, and it's not just a pleasant exception to the unpleasant rule. So, I thought, I need to get people to have multiple interactions, then there's this gradual change over time. People became slowly more and more confident.

So how did you persuade people to have multiple interactions with strangers?

Well, I thought if people don't want to talk to even one stranger, how am I going to get them to talk to many? It didn't seem feasible to ask them to come into the lab every day; I had to let them just get on with it out in the world. So I realised I had to make it fun. Inspired by a colleague,

Try a Little Kindness

I decided that a scavenger hunt might work. I asked people to find someone who was wearing a hat, or someone who was buying a coffee, and talk to them. I didn't want the challenges to be as hard as they are in traditional scavenger hunts. I wanted them to be really easy. I gave people a specific target, and I think that was helpful. Sometimes it's overwhelming to have too much choice, like if you go to the shop and you want to buy some jam, and there's thirty different kinds. How do you choose? It's easier if there's only two!

Yes, it is! What would you say were a couple of your favourite interactions with strangers and how have they affected you?

They are often just little moments, nothing special, but they're still moments to enjoy and cherish, like everyday pleasures. My favourite interaction with a stranger ever was when I had been on BBC Radio 4 *Woman's Hour* in the morning. It was very exciting – I'd been at Broadcasting House in London. Afterwards I was travelling home mid-morning. There are not too many people on the tube at that time. I started talking to this lady, asking, 'How is your day going?' and she responded politely. After a pause she said, 'How's your day been?' So, I said, 'I've had an exciting morning, I've been on *Woman's Hour*.' And she said, 'Oh, really?' And we talked about that a little bit, and then she said, 'Well, actually, I was just at the doctor, and I've just found out that I'm pregnant.' She was on her way back to work, and of course she wouldn't tell anybody, because you don't for a while to make sure everything's okay. But she could tell me because she was never going to see me again. And we shared a hug on the tube. I felt so happy to be able to share that moment with her. It felt really special.

There's this idea about London that I hear so often, that it's an absolute taboo to talk to people on the tube. And you know, it just isn't true anymore – if indeed it ever was! I had to burst through that myth when I started my experiment with kindness too, because many of my interactions happened on the tube.

Yes, ever since I moved to England, I'd been told that you don't talk to people on the tube, but I've had some really nice conversations. I understand that people are tired, they've had a long day, but I think having a conversation is actually really invigorating. If you do it, I think you generally feel better. Humans are fascinating because we sometimes do exactly the opposite of what's good for us. When we get depressed and stressed out, we withdraw from other people. That's exactly the wrong thing to do.

I suppose there's risk involved in talking to strangers, isn't there? I was very interested in your research around us assuming that people aren't going to like us, and how we protect ourselves from that by keeping our distance.

Yes. I teach these 'how to talk to strangers' workshops. In them, I always ask people to think about rejection and what it means, because I think we're quite sensitive to rejection. It makes sense, because it hurts in the same way that physical pain does, it affects the same parts of the brain, and it's crucial to our survival and wellbeing to feel connected and that we belong. So it makes sense that we're sensitive. But perhaps we're overly sensitive. I think we read a lot of things as rejection. And so I always ask people to think about what they think rejection looks like. I ask them: What do you see that makes you conclude that you're being rejected? What does that mean? What else could it mean instead? For example, someone's looking at their watch. It could mean that they're bored, but it could also mean that they have an important meeting that they need to get to, and they'd really like to keep talking to you, but they have to make sure that they have enough time. So, I think you can frame how you're reacting. I think it's just like falling off a horse, you know, they say get right back on. I remember I was on the tube once, and

Try a Little Kindness

I turned to the person on my right and tried to have a little chat, and she was polite, but she got out her book and plugged in her headphones, and I thought all right, so I talked to the person on my left, and we had a really nice chat. I'd like to think that that lady on the right thought, well, that nice chat they're having now, that could have been me. But maybe she didn't feel safe talking to me, or wondered why I was talking to her, or just didn't feel comfortable with it, and that's okay.

I know you are interested in barriers that prevent people from connecting – what are those?

When I started doing this research, I thought, I'll just talk to a lot of people, figure out what they're scared of about talking to strangers, and then figure out how to fix it, and then everybody will talk, and we all live happily ever after . . . but that was very naïve! What I learned is people are worried about so many different things. People worry about their own experience in the conversation, you know: am I going to be bored? Am I going to like the person? How am I going to feel having the conversation?

Then we worry about what are they going to think of me? Are they going to even want to talk to me? Are they going to think I'm weird? Are they going to be bored? Are we going to have enough things to say? What if I offend them? What if they don't understand me? There's just so many things people worry about. I think it's impossible to fix the problem by addressing any single barrier, because then people just worry about something else.

But I think in general it's helpful to realise that we're not necessarily aware of all the negative things that we're telling ourselves. We walk around thinking that we're not very interesting, or that we don't know what we're doing, and those things are not objectively true. What the research tells us is, people like us more than we think, and we tend to be better at talking to strangers than we think we are. If you relied on data like scientists, every single person you know right now, at some point you didn't know them and you managed to talk to them, didn't you? We managed fine, so we have those skills, but we somehow seem to not trust our own social skills. We just think we're rubbish at it, and it's really fascinating, scientifically speaking, because in general, we seem to think we're better than average in almost every way. We think we're better than average drivers, for example. But in terms of social stuff, it's exactly the opposite. We tend to think we're worse than average.

Yes, it's so useful to notice our negative thoughts, and challenge them, to turn them around when they're unhelpful, as they often are.

Yes. And I think to realise that everybody has those negative thoughts can be helpful too. So when I run these 'how to talk to strangers' workshops, I think probably the single most useful thing is for people to understand they're not the only one who's worried.

So how is your research on talking to strangers connected with your kindness research at the University of Sussex?

When this position at the University of Sussex came up to be the Director of the Centre for Research on Kindness, I thought, *Do I do research on kindness? Could I apply for that?* But I had been thinking about how talking to a stranger can sometimes be a pro-social act, an act of kindness in itself, and how there is a benefit to you, as it increases the feeling that people are friendly. From my personal experience of talking to strangers, that's the biggest benefit. There's the momentary fun of having a nice conversation, but I think what it adds up to is so much more important because it makes me feel like I can talk to pretty much anybody, and we have so much in common, and we're going to have a nice chat, and maybe people are generally okay, you know. I mean, there are some terrible people in the world, I'm not denying that. But in general people are okay, and maybe this world isn't so scary and awful. I think that's the biggest benefit of doing this.

Try a Little Kindness

Yes, I agree! I wanted to offer acts of kindness out in the world, but actually, every single time, it was me building up more strength, getting more resilient, getting a bit more hope back.

Yes, I absolutely think that there's plenty of benefits for me. So, there's the benefits that come from an individual interaction, which is sometimes just a moment of joy or learning something new or having a laugh. But more broadly, just this feeling that the world is an okay place. And it's made me feel a lot more confident. I know how to start a conversation with a stranger. I feel like I'm better at keeping conversation going. I feel like that sort of translated into other areas that I would never have imagined, you know. So I feel like I'm more willing to ask someone for help, or I'm more willing to ask a question. I think my instinct is that there's a general social skill set that we use in all sorts of different ways, and I feel like I've built that over time by having these small conversations, and so I benefit from those skills, being a little more confident in those skills. I'm still an introvert, I don't want to go to a party and be stuck in a situation where I have to talk to someone for fifteen minutes, that's still scary.

But that feels really different, doesn't it?

Exactly *(laughs)*. I think what *you* do involves two possibly scary things! You have to approach a stranger and talk to them. And then you're also doing an act of kindness, which is a separate 'What are they going to think about this? How is it going to be received?' moment, you know? So you're doing two things, really.

That's true, though sometimes it was clear that for both of us, me and the stranger, the conversation was the kind thing.

Yes. In The Kindness Test that we conducted at the University of Sussex, when people reported about the most recent act of kindness they received, about 10 per cent of the time it was from a stranger. And when we looked at what those acts are, a lot of them were someone smiling, giving them a compliment, having a chat, being friendly, so it is just those little things that people do see as an act of kindness.

Listening to Gillian confirmed my thoughts about my own experiences while experimenting with kindness — gradually becoming more confident during those first few weeks at talking to strangers, developing some approaches to make it easier and managing to overcome my fears and negative thoughts. It was so helpful to be reminded of how we are all afraid and worried sometimes, that we can all be fragile creatures and that reaching out to each other can only reduce the fears and isolation.

2. SEPTEMBER

Flower Power

Five Acts of Kindness this month:

Day 15: As I was heading for the corner shop for some teabags, I met a woman struggling with very heavy shopping bags. She accepted my offer to help her carry them home. The round trip took one and a half hours. When I got home, I had a well-deserved cuppa.

Day 19: I left a box of chocolates on a doorstep, rang the bell and ran away.

Day 25: I delivered a plate of homemade cakes to my new neighbour. She was astonished.

Day 30: I left an envelope with a fiver at a bar in London Bridge with a note saying, 'Have a drink on me.'

Day 32: I posted a packet of wildflower seeds through a stranger's door with instructions on what kind of flowers they were and where/when is good to plant them.

September arrived, and with it all the familiar feelings and associations. This month has always made me feel tingly with anticipation. Years of school, college and then university terms beginning have drilled this into me — September feels more like the New Year than January.

I'd done a couple of weeks of my kindness mission now and was in my stride, still in the 'honeymoon period' and enjoying recording what I had been up to on Facebook and Twitter. It had been a lark, so far — nerve-wracking, exciting and creative. I was beginning to realise the kinds of things that worked well. And the ones that I enjoyed doing.

So, after my first very positive experience, I felt confident that giving strangers flowers would always be a winner. As botanist and horticulturalist Luther Burbank said, 'Flowers always make people better, happier and more helpful; they are sunshine, food and medicine to the mind.' They made me happy too, reminding me of my grandad and his pride in his chrysanthemums. Giving someone flowers seemed like something anyone would love.

Right at the beginning of September, I went to visit my friend Brett. He runs a beautiful flower stall on Deptford market near the Albany Theatre. He has been there for thirty years. This is usually how our conversation goes.

Me: Are they *insert incorrect flower name here*?
Brett: No, they're *insert correct flower name here*.
Me: Oh. They're lovely. I'll take them.

Brett looks like a cowboy who has hung up his spurs and opted for a more peaceful life among daffodils and freesias. He also looks like, if he was absolutely called upon to do so, he could lasso a bucking bronco, although this prospect is unlikely on the streets of SE8. He is always helpful, assisting his customers as they select bouquets, and wrapping up their cacti. He makes people laugh and remembers their names, and his stall is a fabulous explosion of colour which never fails to brighten my day.

After four offers, he eventually allowed me to buy him a cup of tea in exchange for hanging out at his flower stall to ponder the connection between kindness and flowers. It was nice to sit with him for an hour and witness for myself how happy people seemed as they bought their blooms.

Since my first success I'd been investigating the origins of why we give each other flowers. Here in the UK, the Victorians had a language of flowers – floriography – which meant sending flower-coded messages to

Flower Power

express feelings that could not be said aloud in nineteenth-century society. Flowers were used to say, 'I love you', 'Well done', 'Thank you' or 'Congratulations'. According to Jackie Lacey, floral designer and director of education at the Floriology Institute in Jacksonville, Florida, giving flowers is a way 'for us to speak when there are no words to convey an emotion'.

The sophisticated flower language developed by the Victorians, as well as the ones in the fourteenth-century Ottoman Empire, in ancient Egypt, Greece, Japan, China and many other countries and cultures, seem to have gone by the wayside. But something has remained – an understanding that the gifting of flowers is an expression of love, and is meant as a kindness.

I told Brett all this. I also asked him if he realised that if someone gave you bluebells it meant 'Your letter was received' – and he said no, he certainly didn't realise that. We agreed that these days if someone gives you flowers you can pretty much assume that their intention is positive. Unless it's a wreath with your name on it and you're not dead, in which case you might have cause for concern. I decided that from now on I'd buy all the flowers for my mission from Brett.

I left his stall even more confident, with a bunch of pansies. I gave them away five minutes later to a stranger at the bus stop who loved them.

Over the course of that first year, I gave away flowers many more times, including to my dentist, a waiter, our postie and the refuse collector, with a variety of responses, and I learned a lot from this simple act of kindness. I left flowers on doorsteps, or flowers instead of tips in cafes and restaurants. I gave single flowers to strangers on trains and buses, planted bulbs in forlorn scraps of land all over London after clearing the litter away (and went back to visit them when they had bloomed) and made daisy-chain necklaces for two little girls in the park. But my absolute favourite, for sheer entertainment value, was when I had bought a bunch of sunflowers and was walking through Greenwich looking out for someone to give them to. I eventually offered them to a traffic warden.

'When I saw you approaching me with a massive bunch of sunflowers, I automatically assumed you were going to hit me with them, so I was pleasantly surprised,' he said.

We had a good chat. He told me his job was hard, and that he didn't tell people what he did for a living as it 'was one of those jobs people hate you for'. This man was doing his job to the best of his ability, earning a living, being friendly and courteous to whoever he met. It didn't seem fair. (Though admittedly I don't drive, so this might soften my attitude.)

I thought a lot after that about people in service jobs, public facing, those visible deliverers of sometimes unpleasant or difficult information. The server in the cafe, the receptionist at the doctors, the security guard. I've done those jobs, and I know how hard it can be when people get frustrated and take it out on you because you are the visible representation of their problems.

So that year, I began to ask *everyone* I encountered, 'How are you?' – and this proved hugely effective in beginning what were often meaningful conversations. It helped me feel connected to everyone I met, and was often a really uplifting experience.

Not always, though. Sometimes it was difficult . . .

Day 21. I was going into Boots the chemists to buy eyeliner, still deciding what to do for my act of kindness today. When I got to the counter, I started chatting to the woman serving on the till.

Me: How are you?
Sad Lady in Boots: Well, to be honest, I've had better weeks.
Me: Oh no, really?
Sad Lady in Boots: Yes, I have had better. I just say to myself, 'There's always someone worse off than you,' and that helps me to get out of bed in the morning, but yes, it's been better.
Me: Oh no. I'm sorry to hear that.

Flower Power

I left the shop. Outside the shop there was a flower and plant stall. I scanned it for something to cheer her up. I'd already begun carrying around a few homemade cards, envelopes and packets of sweets in my bag for 'emergency kindness' situations, so I quickly wrote a card saying, 'These flowers are to wish you a better week' and I bought her a flowering plant from the stall. Then I ran back inside and gave it to her. I was a bit nervous, so all my words tumbled out in a bit of a rush:

Me: Hellothisisforyousorryyouarehavingasadweekiamtryingtodo somethingniceeverydayforpeopleidontknowiambernadette.
PAUSE (*while she digested the speedy communication*)
Sad Lady in Boots: That's so nice. You are very nice.
Me: Oh, thanks.

She was very sweet, but as I left, she looked as though she was about to cry. That wasn't the effect I'd been hoping for.

I learned a lot from the interaction, although it took a while to process it. One of the main lessons was: if you ask everyone you meet how they are, then sooner or later you might get an answer that is more than you bargained for. I really appreciated her honesty. I'm glad she told me how she was feeling. But what I noticed was how much I felt it too. It was not comfortable. Walking into Boots, I'd been happy, even quite pleased with myself, and after that interaction I felt tearful and sad, and worried that my flowers hadn't done much to help.

This was the first time I decided to look into how my brain's neurological responses might be affected by the activity I was undertaking. And how this might be impacting me, as well as others.

I came across the neuroscientist Marco Iacoboni, whose work examines the type of brain cell that 'mirrors' what we perceive from others. These 'mirror neurons' enable us to understand other people's actions, intentions and feelings. Mirror neurons exist in many areas of our brains, and they fire up both when we experience emotion and when we see others experiencing an emotion. When we see someone being sad, for example, our mirror neurons fire and that allows us to experience the same feeling. In his book *Mirroring People*, Iacoboni writes about how these mirror neurons 'help us to be empathic and fundamentally attuned to other people. This is perhaps the most important finding of all, and it is a beautiful one.'

So this is what empathy is — experiencing first hand the pain of someone else. According to physicist Michio Kaku, these mirror neurons are probably essential for our evolution — the glue that once held our tribes together.

More reading brought me to some research conducted at Berkeley University in California. One sentence jumped out: 'Having empathy doesn't necessarily mean we'll want to help someone in need, though it's often a vital first step toward compassionate action.'

I realised that this was what had happened when I met the Sad Lady in Boots. I felt sad seeing she was sad, and I was moved to try to do something to help or to cheer her up. I also realised that I experience this a lot. This is why I often find the news so overwhelming, and why I can't watch dramas set in hospital wards or documentaries about war. It's something that social psychologist Megan Shen explores in her work. 'The most significant payoff to suffering is compassion,' she says, 'not just resilience.'

So maybe for all of us there's an opportunity to make meaning of our own suffering, and to see it as a gift that makes us more able to connect with other people's suffering.

Flowers are not completely unproblematic, either — something that dawned on me when I gave a woman in Wandsworth a bunch of roses. I had bought them in haste from a supermarket, and I chose her because I saw to my delight that they'd match her outfit. She was very happy with them. But as I handed them to her, I saw the label said 'Produce of

Flower Power

Kenya.' Then I noticed they were wrapped in single-use plastic. For the first time I considered the kindness of this flower-giving. The flowers were not kind to the environment – what with the plastic, and the fossil fuels needed to get them here. Perhaps instead I should be looking for flowers grown locally.

Later, when I was on tour with my theatre show telling the story of my year of kindness, I recreated the flower-giving moment as a bit of fun. I randomly chose someone in the audience to give some flowers to. Afterwards I would ask the recipient, 'In the spirit of scientific investigation and data gathering, could you just tell me if, after I gave you the flowers, did you feel a) better than before, b) the same or c) worse than before?'

Almost everyone said 'a', because there's a certain amount of pressure to answer that way, of course. But once or twice people did say 'c'. One woman told me why: 'They make me feel worse because they are dead, and that makes me sad.' I admired her honesty and have never given away cut flowers since. Instead, I endeavour to give flowering plants in pots (which can carry on living), in peat-free compost (to help support the unique biodiversity of peatlands and keep the carbon they store locked within them) and grown locally (reducing transport emissions). It's still just as fun, and it feels much better.

The simple act of giving someone flowers changed and deepened as I became more aware of how far-reaching and radical kindness can be. It seems fitting here to consider the etymology of 'radical': it comes from the Latin *radix* meaning 'root'. So 'radical' means 'relating to the root of the matter' – and I think to be radical in this instance is to pay careful attention to every part of the act.

The gifting of flowers can become more than a cellophane tube filled with imported roses thrust into the hands of a woman in a bar in Wandsworth who I thought looked a bit sad. Instead, maybe it would be better to pick her some wildflowers from my garden and tie them with string, or to give her some bulbs or seeds.

Then if she wanted to, she could plant them. And when they bloomed, seeing them could be a reminder of the day a stranger came into her bar and they spoke together about life's ups and downs and about how maybe everything would be ok.

Kamilah McInnis is a BBC multi-media journalist, producer, presenter and musician whom I met first during lockdown on the online festival of kindness KindFest, initiated by Susie Hills (more about Susie and KindFest later). Kamilah's powerful story gave me confidence and courage. Here we are talking about flowers, mental health and the importance of kindness.

The Language of Flowers
with Kamilah McInnis

First of all, could you share your beautiful 'flower story' with me?

Yeah, well, because I am naturally quite an outgoing, talkative person, who likes to use my arms a lot, people think I'm always happy. But there's this other side to me. I've suffered on and off with depression for years, and it seems to come back every year, particularly in the winter.

I first started taking antidepressants aged seventeen. I didn't even really know then what depression was. But I knew that it was something that was quite taboo in all society, and there is also a stigma around it within the black communities, although this is improving. I think this may be because we have extra things to worry about, like racism and discrimination and things like that. We've always just had to be resilient. Poor mental health has in cases been seen as something that doesn't affect black communities, and we have been underrepresented in studies and research. We have been missing from conversations. I had a white therapist who didn't understand me, and assumed that because I was from a single parent household that that's where my issues came from, and she also completely misunderstood my culture. And that's why people have asked for black therapists in the past, because there was this misunderstanding.

I think that's a prime example. I had another friend who was sectioned, and they recovered while in the mental health hospital, and then said, I think I'm ready to be released now. And they said, No, you're not. You threatened someone last week and you were violent. When actually, they'd mixed my friend up with a different black patient. So, these are true stories which need to be considered too.

For myself, I reached a point a few years ago where I just accepted that was the way that my brain worked, and that encouraged me to turn my pain into power, as a way of supporting other people around me. I didn't know how to deal with it, and I didn't want other people to feel the way that I felt, because it's awful when I'm going through it. And so, I guess I became more comfortable, not to say that I accepted it, it's not my identity. It is just something that I experience, and I experience a kind of existential crisis, and wonder what my purpose is. And that can then lead to depression, so I reached the point where I felt I was ready to talk about it, because it had been happening to me, and I wanted to talk about the prevalence of it. And then at a very, very, low point for me, something incredible happened.

I think you described it before as a particularly bad day...

It was an awful time. During that period, around 2020, I'd had multiple suicide attempts, and I had just been going into work the next day afterwards. People didn't know what I was going through. I went for a walk outside because I felt I just didn't know what I was doing with my life. I didn't know if I should be here anymore. I found myself thinking, 'What is the point of this?' I was in a mental health crisis, and I was crying.

That's why it was so powerful, and so magical, and so amazing, when I looked down and there was a bunch of flowers there, because I was at one of the lowest points in my life and it was so strange I couldn't believe it. There was this tag attached to the flowers, saying, 'This is a free gift for you from The Flower Bank.'

So straight away I looked up The Flower Bank and discovered that it was this tiny charity based in North London where I'm from, run by this amazing woman called Ursula Stone. The charity repurposes old flowers that are being thrown out of supermarkets and wholesalers, brings them back to life and leaves them on the street for people to find, and donates them to old people's homes, community centres, all those kinds of places.

After that I did this piece with her, because I wanted to shed light on how kindness can be beneficial to your mental health. So I called the piece 'Kindness Can Help Save Lives', because it can in some cases! And it was one of the BBC News most watched videos of the day. It was shared countless times. And I got hundreds of messages from people thanking me, and telling me how much it touched them, and how comforting they found it. At the time I felt it saved my life, although I didn't go into detail about that in the piece because I was the journalist reporting on it. I also included the group Stronger Together in that piece – they are a group of people with mental health struggles, who go out and write beautiful uplifting notes and leave them on bridges to deter people who are having suicidal thoughts.

What incredible discoveries! It is so encouraging to hear about these kinds of initiatives. And what would you say was the impact of finding those flowers for you personally?

I do think me finding those flowers that day gave me a sense of purpose, because I discovered the world of kindness through putting out that piece. I was contacted by Susie Hills, the founder of KindFest, and she asked me to be a host. I've had all these amazing opportunities.

I was invited to go back to my university to talk to the students about getting into journalism, and I remember talking to my friends and joking

Flower Power

about it, because I can still, even when I'm depressed, have a joke, and I said, 'They're going to ask me, should I get into journalism? I'm going to say, no, it was the worst idea of my life.'

Afterwards I went out for dinner with my friend. We both got pizzas, the chef had made me this heart shaped pizza, and he just said, 'Here you go! This is for you.' And that was all in the same period. In the space of a week, I'd had a suicide attempt, found those flowers, gone back to my university to give a talk and got a heart-shaped pizza. I'd never had anything like that happen to me before.

I'm so glad you had those positive experiences after such a hugely difficult time. I always say that kindness is magic, because it has the power to transform situations and people.

There we go! We've got power of kindness on our side!

As I learned from talking to Kamilah, even small acts of kindness might be powerful enough to save a life. They can make someone's day, restore people's faith in each other and give hope. When the self-doubt comes calling, I hold on to this, still.

As Mark Twain said, 'Kindness is the language that the deaf can hear and the blind can see.' A simple gift of flowers, or some other small act of kindness can communicate 'Don't give up', 'The world is full of beauty', 'You are cared for', 'You are not alone', 'Things will get better', 'There are amazing and kind people in the world' and more. Kindness is a language that in September of 2011 I was just beginning to learn.

3. OCTOBER

Be Kind to All Kinds

> *Five acts of kindness this month:*
>
> **Day 49**: I helped some tourists find their way on the tube by walking with them to the platform they needed. Then I gave them my number and told them to call if they needed help.
>
> **Day 56**: My birthday. I left a homemade card with a nice message inside on a seat inside the National Portrait Gallery. About five minutes later, I saw a lady pick it up and smile.
>
> **Day 58**: I placed a bookmark with a kind message inside a book in a charity shop.
>
> **Day 64**: I took some vegan cakes down to St Paul's Occupy London camp. The man thanked me and told me that they have loads of cakes and bread but no vegetables, so the next day I went back and took carrots.
>
> **Day 65**: During a monthly storytelling show in East London, I found out someone in the audience had had her bike stolen, so I gave her a fiver towards another.

I was, most days, having a great time now. The people I encountered were usually receptive and friendly, intrigued and interested when I explained my mission. They were often eager to talk to me about how the world was full of kindness if you stopped and allowed yourself to pay attention.

I realised that the truly powerful combination was not only carrying out acts of kindness, but noticing when I received or witnessed them. So I began to concentrate not only on my own acts, but on all the small acts of kindness I saw in a single day. It was as if I had been invited to see the world in an entirely new way, a kind of re-enchantment. It did seem to me that the world was full of wonderfully kind, compassionate and caring actions happening all the time.

I noticed the other stuff too – people being grumpy or rude to each other, terrible things happening all over the world – but I also saw there was more of the good stuff than we are led to believe. I was gaining more confidence in the ability of me and of other human beings to be kind to each other, and that felt good. But, as it turned out, this month became less about people and more about the more-than-human earthlings and the world we share with them.

Early on in October I shared a post on social media about how I had fed a dog half of my croissant even though I was very hungry, and asked, 'Does this count as a kindness?' Now the answer to that is probably, not really, if you are asking whether you should feed a dog with a perhaps delicate digestion a buttery bread. But in terms of does it count if the kindness is not directed towards a human, then hell, yes!

It was a rhetorical question. I knew what I thought – I wanted to see what friends and colleagues thought. Everyone responded with yes (as well as lots of people telling me not to give dogs croissants, which I promise I haven't done since).

Later that day I read something Einstein had said: 'A human being is part of a whole, called by us the "Universe", a part limited in time and space. He experiences himself, his thoughts and feelings, as something separated from the rest – a kind of optical delusion of his consciousness. This delusion is a kind of prison for us, restricting us to our personal desires and to affection for a few persons nearest us. Our task must be to free ourselves from this prison by widening our circles of compassion to embrace *all living creatures and the whole of nature in its beauty*.' And I agreed. I was determined to include all animals and the natural environment in my kindness mission.

Be Kind to All Kinds

One day, I got chatting to a woman at the traffic lights at the bottom of Deptford High Street. I patted her dog and said he was cute. And she explained that her experience of love and kindness came from her dog: 'I like dogs better than people – they are easier to get along with. People are so cruel. No dog has ever hurt me like a person has,' she said.

As I moved through the year, many people experiencing homelessness told me the same – that animals can be the givers as well as the receivers of much kindness.

Later that month, on the way to a talk at Somerset House, I saw lots of teeny mice scampering up the stairs and I fed them cupcakes. After reading about the damage caused to wildlife by plastic waste, I started taking a bag out so that I could clear up rubbish from my local park when I was walking through. I began filling the bird feeders in the park. I reconsidered the ideas of animal rights that my younger self had been so passionate about.

I had been a vegetarian for decades by now. It had started when, for a whole magical year, when I was eleven, we lived in the idyll known then as East Burton in Dorset. Our stepdad was working away, and we very rarely saw him, so my sister and I were safe and living in a beautiful place with our lovely mum. The summer of that year we went to the local fair, and much fun was had by me and my sister throwing wet sponges at adults in stocks and trying to throw hoops over things to win other things. I got a gold-plated pocket watch in a lucky dip, which felt like a miracle to me. I couldn't imagine people so rich that they could donate ancient gold watches just like that.

It was at that fair that I found out where pork came from. First, I watched people having fun trying to catch cute and slippery little piglets. Then I saw the piglets hanging up dead by their trotters. I'd never made the connection before, not so clearly. It was very distressing. Not least because I really loved the taste of bacon, and I knew in that moment I couldn't bring myself to eat it again. All my favourite books as a kid had been about animals. I'd wallpapered the walls of my bedroom with pages from *World of Wildlife* magazine. I loved our cat Mitzi. It took me until I was fifteen years old, when I was able to cook for myself and buy some of my own food using money from a Saturday job, to give up eating meat entirely, and I missed it to begin with. But I couldn't reconcile eating it with the little piglets and other animals having to sacrifice their happy lives for me to tuck into a Sunday roast. To this day I have never cooked meat.

These days being vegetarian isn't such a big deal. But in the 1980s, it was still a little odd, and as for vegans, well, they were just wackos who 'knitted their own yogurt', as my English teacher joked. When I told my nana I was vegetarian, she said, 'That's okay, I'll just make you a ham omelette.' Nana knew that ham was meat, of course, but she thought I'd meant I wouldn't eat great big slabs of meat, or anything that looked like the animal that had died. For my working-class grandparents who had endured rationing, it was an eccentric choice, but they really tried to accommodate what seemed to them like very bizarre requests, and I loved them for it.

When I was sixteen, I joined the Hampshire hunt saboteurs, travelling with a load of anarchist crusties in the back of a transit van to try to save a fox from a gruesome death. I was often dressed in a fake-fur coat and had long blonde hair extensions which kept snagging on the barbed wire we had to navigate, so that particular form of activism didn't last long. I was vaguely disapproved of, and to be honest wearing bright red lipstick and fake eyelashes did seem a little incongruous. The hunters themselves were terrifying. Their horses were massive and steaming, and they exuded confidence and arrogance, that kind of upper-middle-class swagger which I hadn't encountered before and couldn't get used to. (I have since met many fabulous upper-middle-class folks who utilise any swagger they may have magnificently and charmingly, but back then I associated it entirely with fox murdering and extreme rudeness.)

Be Kind to All Kinds

In those days, people who still ate meat said baffling things to me like 'Don't you worry about the vegetables suffering?' or 'I love meat too much to give it up' (*You have no idea how much I loved bacon*, I'd think) or, most challengingly, 'Why don't you focus on human suffering when there is so much?' This last one stopped me in my tracks and made me ask myself, 'Is this because I don't love people as much? Is there something wrong with me?' But that just wasn't and isn't true. Caring for people and caring for animals were connected in ways I felt rather than understood intellectually, and I drew early inspiration from animal-rights activist George Thorndike Angell, who said, 'I am sometimes asked why do you spend so much of your time and money talking about kindness to animals when there is so much cruelty to men? I answer I am working at the roots.'

That's how it *felt* – that cruelty to animals and cruelty to people and cruelty to the planet were inseparable causes. I did and still do try to speak out and stand up for those who for many complex reasons do not get heard. Animals are among these. As writer Alice Walker said, 'Animals can communicate quite well. And they do. And generally speaking, they are ignored.'

I'd noticed how often they were segregated, these causes that to me seemed so interconnected, and how angry it makes some people if you dare to talk about the rights of animals. A friend told me this was because they felt like their lives were hard enough without having 'a reduced life in which you are told you are not allowed so many things you enjoy'.

I found out my friend Roxanna was vegan. She didn't try to persuade me of anything, she didn't tell me I wasn't doing enough by being a vegetarian, I didn't feel judged or disapproved of by her, but her quiet example made me realise I hadn't thought about my own reasons for becoming vegetarian since I first made that decision, and maybe it was time to reconsider it, and go further. On her recommendation I eventually watched *Earthlings*, a film about factory farms and other places of animal suffering, narrated by Joaquin Phoenix. I had been putting it off because I knew it would require changes of me that I wasn't sure I was ready to make. Before I even got halfway through, I knew I couldn't eat dairy anymore if I really want to commit to being 'kind to all kinds'. I followed Roxanna's lead: I didn't announce it, I just got on with it. I have continued to try to educate myself more about the connection between food and kindness since.

But whatever *you* eat, please don't think I am trying to persuade you of anything in this chapter. I honestly believe we are all doing our best in the circumstances we are in. That different things are important to different people at different times. That there are huge cultural, socio-economic, family and just personal differences that affect our choices of what we eat. I have the luxury of having time to cook: not everyone has that. I also love cooking, I always have, and I don't find it that difficult. I've never felt ill or tired from eating no meat or dairy (I'm aware from friends who have tried it that some people do), I have access to a nearby fruit and veg market, and these days I usually have enough money to buy the food I want. Although I am from a cultural background of meat-eating, milk-drinking people, no one has felt offended or rejected because of my decisions to stop eating it. I live in a time and a place where vegan/vegetarian options are plentiful.

To help me understand the connection between kindness to animals and the natural world and kindness to my fellow humans, I got in touch with Compassion in World Farming, a wonderful lobbying animal-welfare organisation that campaigns against export of live animals, certain methods of slaughter and all systems of factory farming. Philip Lymbery is the CEO and has a much deeper and broader understanding of these subjects than me. Here's our chat – I hope it inspires you as much as it inspired me.

Be Kind to All Kinds

We Are All Interconnected
with Philip Lymbery

I know that your work is all about considering kindness to animals, in particular farm animals. And your website states that you believe that 'a society can be judged by the way in which it feeds its people and treats its animals'. If that's the case, then how would you say we're doing now?

Pretty badly is how we're doing at the moment I think, on the societal scale of how kindly we're treating animals. Most of them are kept in factory farms in Britain and Europe, despite us being a nation of so-called animal lovers. We've got a long way to go before we can say that we're putting kindness into action.

You've written about how factory farming came to be in the first place; could you speak about that a little?

Well, I trace the origins of factory farming back to the Dust Bowl era of the American Midwest in the 1930s, when the American government encouraged settlers to set up a homestead on the plains, which had previously been home to tens of millions of bison and the indigenous Americans that lived alongside them. The settlers found deeply fertile soil that had become enriched by centuries of being nurtured by nature. They farmed on the land and got record crop yields from it, but the soil became depleted, as it was no longer being fertilised by the bison that had lived there. And after the Wall Street Crash of 1929, the homesteaders were suddenly getting only half the amount for the food that they were producing, which was quite a knock.

So, what do you do in a situation where you only get half the money for your produce? Well, you use more land and produce twice as much, of course, only what that does is exacerbate the oversupply and it also left vast amounts of land area of soil now bare, as the prairie grass that once held it together and protected it from the elements was no longer there. And when the winds came, they picked up the soil and took it in huge dust clouds, high as a mountain range and up to 200 miles long, and it would sweep across the plains, turning day into night, and people feared for their lives. This was a very dramatic moment in history that shows what happens if we don't look after the soil. Shortly afterwards, wheat and other commodity grains became so cheap and plentiful that farmers decided that they may as well start feeding them to their animals. And that's where factory farming started, essentially, and that became a new way of keeping animals in confinement, feeding them on these new, cheap grain sources.

By the time you get to the end of the Second World War bomb factories were decommissioned, and instead were put to work as fertiliser producers, using ammonia in a different way. Chemical pesticides too emerged at this time. The German regime has been testing deadly chemicals on insects that they were then going to use to kill people in the war, although they never actually deployed these chemicals in the battlefield. But the Allies took this technology and started to use it to kill insects in the farming environment, so deadly pesticides were born.

That intensification of agriculture got exported from America to the UK and Europe after the Second World War, and we've been living with that legacy ever since. Factory farming is the biggest cause of animal cruelty on the planet. It is also the biggest driver of wildlife declines – and the biggest waste of food, because feeding human-edible crops to farmed animals means that most of the food value of that crop gets wasted in conversion to meat, milk and eggs, in terms of both calories and protein, ironically. And in that transaction, we waste 4 billion people's worth of food every year. That's enough to feed half of humanity. We do not have a problem producing enough food in the world. We just waste so much of it, and the biggest form of food waste on the planet is in feeding human-edible grains to animals kept in abject misery in factory farms.

Be Kind to All Kinds

Let's put it another way — if we were kind to the animals and gave them the ability to live a decent life where they could experience the joy of being pasture-fed or free ranging and these kind of more nature-friendly ways of keeping animals, it would be better for our environment, it would be better for the nutritional value of our food. It would be healthier. It would be less of a pandemic risk. And it would protect our soil, too, which is seriously in decline due to the use of pesticides, artificial fertilisers and cages in factory farming. It comes down this: being unkind to farmed animals is undermining the future for our children, and for our society.

So what could regular citizens do to help our farmers and our food producers create a different kind of world for farm animals, for farmland and for themselves?

I think the starting point is that there are beautiful, life-affirming, kind and compassionate solutions at hand that can help us rebuild the future for people, animals and the planet, and I summarise those as the three Rs. The first is to **regenerate** the countryside by doing away with factory farming and, instead, having nature-friendly farming. The second is to **rethink** protein and to reduce our overall meat and dairy intake as a nation and as a society, because we eat too much meat and dairy as it stands. If we carry on overeating meat and dairy, our food alone could trigger catastrophic climate change, given the amount of greenhouse gases coming from their production. So, there is a need eat more plant-based foods and less, but better-quality, meat and dairy.

The third is **rewilding** the soil, which we can do by bringing animals back as part of mixed rotational farms, where they can live their best life with the sun on their backs, helping to fertilise the soil, providing harvests based on kindness and compassion to animals and thereby people.

But to come back to your question, what can we, as concerned citizens, do? Well, we can seize the power of our plates three times a day.

By eating more plants, and less and better meat and dairy. By better, I mean choosing more regenerative agroecological food sources, where the animals have been kept better, where nature is looked after better and which provide us as people with more nutritious food. So, choosing pasture-fed, free-range or organic food is the way that we, as concerned citizens, can create a better future for us all.

Are there any farms in the UK doing things in the right way?

Yes, there's plenty. For example, there's a farm called Kingsclere Estates near Basingstoke, in Hampshire, run by Tim May, overlooking Watership Down. It was an intensive arable farm, producing lots of grain, much of which was feeding factory-farmed animals. And it was producing that grain in monoculture intensification, using chemical pesticides and fertilisers. Tim took it over from his father, and what he found was that it didn't matter how much extra he used chemicals, pesticides and fertilisers, his yields were declining, and the reason for that was because his soil health was declining.

So he resisted the temptation to phone the chemical man and ask for something stronger. He put the chemicals away in the barn, which saved him £700 per hectare. And this is a big farm, ten times bigger than the national average farm size in Britain. Then he brought farmed animals back, and they started to move around the farm in mixed rotations, fed only on grass, no grain or other intensification, all entirely cage free. And now his farm is seeing a restoration of soil health, and it's seen wildlife come flooding back. His cattle are kept in beautiful pasture conditions, and they are followed in the rotation by sheep, then pigs, then chickens, and then crops. This is the rotation of life as it should be. He is showing in an agricultural microcosm what the future looks like, an example of regenerative farming, a beautiful, life-affirming, kind and compassionate way of producing food in ways that respect animal as sentient beings, creatures that can feel pain, suffer or alternatively enjoy life if we let them.

Be Kind to All Kinds

So what can be done to overcome whatever challenges there might be for there to be more farms like that?

It's down to pioneers, people who are willing to take a risk and break the mould like Tim May and other regenerative farmers. It's taken their leadership and courage to show that there is an alternative way and to make it work. And it's not easy, because there are huge companies, a small handful of big agricultural companies: pharmaceutical companies, fertiliser companies, pesticide companies and chemical companies who have grown very, very rich from the fact that for seventy years farmers have been persuaded to buy needless and harmful chemicals for their land. The farmers haven't benefited from this, as they've been going out of business as if farming is going out of fashion. It's these big agricultural companies that have benefited, many of them run by people who really don't understand the countryside, aided and abetted by governments. So we've been locked into a toxic situation, and we need pioneers. And thankfully, there is a growing band of renegade farmers, as I call them, who are daring to do things differently and to make it work. And they're inspiring people throughout the country and throughout the world.

So we need changes in government policy. We need to lobby our MPs, and we need to communicate with them at a local level, about changes that we want wherever we live, and champion MPs who are supporting change.

We do. We need government subsidies and policies to get behind the new regenerative ways of producing food, and we can all take part by pressuring our governments. We can also pressure supermarkets to offer more nature-friendly food.

And buy nature-friendly food when we see it and when we are able to. On your website I saw to look out for food labelled as free range, organic, pasture for life or RSPCA assured.

Yes. The food we choose has a direct impact on how farm animals live, so it's really important.

The great thing about farmed animals kept in regenerative farm systems is that it's in harmony with nature, and with the animals' nature. I don't just mean the fact that it brings back pollinating insects, birds, bats and all sorts of other creatures to the wild part of the landscape, but it also appeals to the intrinsic nature of the farmed animals so that they can be themselves. It means that pigs can be piggy again, chickens can be chickeny and cows can be cowy, if you like! It means that the animals can express their natural behaviours: they can run, flap, jump, scratch, peck and nuzzle the ground. They can be themselves and live their best lives.

Animals don't ask for much. They just ask to be put back into their natural environment rather than having an artificial, impoverished environment thrust upon them. And in regenerative farms animals are in the environment where they can live their best lives and enjoy the freedom of living.

And is this revolution in farming driven by kindness?

Yes, I would say it is. And being kind now is an absolute necessity. In these times of growing anxiety around climate change, the collapse of nature and the fear of new pandemics and disease, being kind to everyone around us is vital. But it's also important to realise that we are all in a 'one health' environment, which means that being kind to people means also being kind to animals and the environment, because we're all interconnected. So, if we are going to overcome those planetary emergencies that are bearing down on us, we've got to be kind. We need to embrace the beautiful, life-affirming, kind and compassionate solutions that are at hand to achieve food for the future, to address the climate emergency, the collapse of nature and warding off future health pandemics.

Be Kind to All Kinds

How optimistic do you feel? Do you see these changes as a possibility, and do you remain hopeful that we can get there?

I do remain hopeful that we will be kind, and that big change will come about because of it. The one thing I can guarantee is that big change is inevitable. The way that we're doing things now will be the ruination of society. It essentially delivers us to an unliveable planet. So that is why kindness is the way forward to avoid that catastrophic future, that failure of human society, to move away from the current situation where essentially we're mortgaging the future with no ability to pay. So yeah, let's be kind and we will address the climate emergency. We will turn around the current collapse of nature. We will ward off future pandemics and we'll stop being cruel to animals. And in this way, we will be kinder to people, too.

You tell a story in your book about your dog Duke, one that illustrates how animals 'have curiosity, express kinship, form friendships, and therefore can experience pleasure and playing as we do'. I think it's important for people to notice that.

We had Duke at ten weeks old as a rescue, and I'd like to think that bringing him up with kindness and respect and teaching him kindness in his interactions with other creatures, has helped him to form a kinship with so many different species. The cows are a good example. They were a new herd that had never met Duke before. They were in a field the other side of the river, but they saw Duke, and they all came one by one across the river. Duke went up to them, gingerly at first, and then suddenly they were all touching noses and licking – which is that age-old way for animals to express kinship and connectivity.

Philip's commitment to a kinder future for farm animals is so encouraging. Our conversation made me sure to my bones that one day we will look back at this time when we caused so much unnecessary suffering and cruelty to so many sentient beings as utter madness. There is a better way, a kinder way.

Cruelty to animals is incomprehensible to me, but I do understand the strange disconnect that comes with cooing at lambs one minute and then eating them for Sunday roast the next. We all do that to some extent. We ignore the cruelties and injustices endemic in things which bring us comfort and pleasure. Like who made our trainers and under what conditions, or where our rubbish ends up. These are difficult things to discuss. People don't want to be made to feel guilty. And why should they? We all indulge in a bit of 'cognitive dissonance' from time to time.

But what if instead of turning away and resisting change because we think it will be hard, we face facts and help each other to realise that a fairer, kinder society doesn't mean less fun or pleasure – but more? With food, it's trying out all the delicious and nutritious alternatives. Not feeling guilty, as that won't change anything, but feeling curious.

Since the very first day of my year of kindness, I have done as much as possible to be kind to people, place, and planet and to support others who are doing so too. Such as Navdeep Deol, the current chair of the Board of Trustees for the National Park City Foundation. Navdeep is from Hounslow, West London and began litter-picking out of a deep sense of frustration about rubbish and fly tipping around his neighbourhood. This was shared by other local volunteers who joined in, but it was difficult to maintain momentum as there was little public recognition for what they were doing and no real improvement in the root of the problem. Yet this group of volunteers – the Heston Action Group or HAG – is still going strong six years later, now inspired more by the positive impact that their actions have on nature, protecting wildlife from litter embedded in the soil and stopping it from entering rivers and seas, than by tidying up the streets or local park for neighbours. As he told himself, *I'm doing this for Mr Fox and Mr Hedgehog, and I'm doing this so the robin doesn't get stuck in litter and so that the dogs don't get snarled up in plastic.* This narrative of serving nature was so powerful that eventually he noticed more volunteers coming to events and regular volunteers becoming more engaged and adventurous. They have since gone on to create new habitats for biodiversity, a tree nursery and to run school events at the local HAG community garden. And ultimately there has been a positive impact on people too: being part of a larger movement with an important purpose has connected like-minded neighbours, helping stave off loneliness and isolation and encouraging them to feel more positive about the place. 'The people who volunteer with us at the community garden smile a lot,' he tells me.

Being disconnected from nature is impossible when you consider we are part of nature. So, if we love and want to be kind to nature, then that love, and kindness, must include ourselves. As Dr Sharon Blackie says in her brilliant Substack *The Art of Enchantment*: 'Giving up on our species just isn't an option. If we give up on humanity, we give up on ourselves, and the world that shelters us, and the other-than-humans that share that world with us. We give up on everything, and that's just not a good place to live from.' Overwhelm about climate change, and the rage and grief that can accompany the fear, are present for so many of us. But there is always something we can do, however small. I still feed the wild birds every day; I'm the 'guardian' for a local street tree — in charge of watering it and monitoring its health; I still volunteer as a tree-planting supervisor at Trees for Cities; and I am almost completely vegan.

I've been taught by the birds tangled in plastic that rubbish is harmful to the world; by my dog's allergies to the chemicals sprayed on the grass in the park that organic is better; by seeing how gleefully cows skip about when they are outside living their best lives that that is where they should be.

Conversations on Kindness

As for the trees that provide oxygen so I can breathe, and the world with its sunsets and sunrises and rainbows and crashing waves and clouds like cathedrals and bees with sticky legs emerging from foxgloves, all of it is gifting me beauty and wonder at every moment, and they are all my kin, my teachers, allies and companions too. There is so much to be grateful for and to fight for in this still-beautiful world we live in. It is uplifting to understand how interconnected everything is. It shows us that all our actions matter, and all our actions are powerful.

As for those money-making, pollution-spewing, suffering-creating industries we are reliant on — is there another way? Is a kinder way possible? I believe it is.

4. NOVEMBER

Another Day in Paradise

> *Five acts of kindness this month:*
>
> **Day 76:** I gave a lottery ticket to a stranger at a photography exhibition in Soho. Chose a man wearing an eccentric and sensational jacket.
>
> **Day 78:** I gave a book of Christmas ghost stories to a man I met on the number 47 bus.
>
> **Day 80:** I sent a gift through the post to a stranger as nominated by a friend on Facebook. It contained: one lucky penny, a rubber duck, a rose bath bomb, body lotion, a heart-shaped balloon, Scooby Doo fizzy sweets, chocolates, glitter, a feather and a card saying, 'Make a wish.'
>
> **Day 87:** I visited a local care home to offer some homemade cakes that couldn't be accepted 'for health and safety reasons'. So I gave them to my neighbour's grandson who happened to be hanging out of the window.
>
> **Day 91:** I saw an old man struggling with his bags so I helped him. 'You're just trying to get to know me, you crafty cow!' he said.

This month my acts of kindness became a kind of ramshackle street magic, like leaving sweet notes with love from 'the fairies' on park benches. The creativity and mischief of these acts of kindness really helped sustain me. It was a joy to make these things and to think up these ideas, as if suddenly I had given myself permission to realise all those wild creative ideas I'd had for so long. As social scientist and Harvard professor Arthur C. Brooks wrote, 'The best way of trying to change the world is the one that will offer you happiness too.' For me that meant creativity, fun and imagination.

Conversations on Kindness

I was ever vigilant for opportunities to offer kindness, and always prepared with some kind of gift in case the opportunity to help someone in some way didn't present itself. I began regularly carrying around with me chocolates, sweets, books carefully wrapped in tissue paper and ribbon, handwritten poems, packets of wildflower seeds. I give these small gifts away randomly to strangers in shops, cafes, libraries and at bus stops.

However, as well as shoppers, commuters, students, joggers, stall holders, posties, graffiti artists and all the other good folk who make our streets lively and vibrant, there are always those who spend more time there than they might like to: people experiencing homelessness.

A key rule for the year had been, 'Thou must never say no if someone asks thou for money.' I just hadn't paid attention before this year to how often this happens, via emails, posts on socials or in person. But this year, that changed. Not every unhoused person I met asked for money, and I didn't always have cash on me when someone did, but I started to pay greater attention to just how much need there was.

One chilly November day, I was waiting to meet a friend in Spitalfields when she texted to say she was running late. I got chatting to a man holding a cardboard sign saying, 'Homeless and hungry, please help me if you can' who had asked me if I had any change.

I hadn't got any cash, but I asked him how he was. He said not bad, and asked me in return what I was doing. When I explained he said, 'I'll wait with you, so you're not on your own.' I suggested he come with me for a coffee while I waited. He seemed stunned that I asked. There was a chain coffee shop nearby, and we sat outside at one of the tables. It was getting dark, and the light from the inside part of the shop spilled onto the pavement.

We introduced ourselves. His name was Mark. When the server came and I asked him what he wanted, he said, 'I don't know, just coffee' and we talked a bit about how overwhelming so many choices can be. I felt

Another Day in Paradise

immediately and deeply conscious of the privileges I don't even notice I have. Like feeling welcome in most places. Being able to buy a coffee. Knowing where I was sleeping that night, and that place being safe, welcoming and warm. Secure housing. As well as the confidence to sit at a table in a café without the slightest fear that I might be asked to leave. Mark had none of these.

He told me that sitting there he realised he'd not been 'inside' before, and by that he meant that he had not been invited into places where 'regular people go'. We talked a lot, and as the sky turned to the magic vivid blue of dusk, he told me how ashamed he was, of the mistakes he had made, and how he was trying to improve his life so he could get back into his son's life. Right now he stayed away, even though he knew where his son was, as he didn't want to embarrass him.

He was saving up, trying to find somewhere more permanent to live, so that he could look into getting work. He used to work in kitchens, and he had 'done building sites too'. He told me he slept standing up in a wardrobe in an abandoned building in Whitechapel and that he had to be careful because some dangerous people were in there, addicts who were desperate and might rob you or just people who were 'not well and might hurt you'. He didn't drink or do drugs: he understood why people did, but drinking had caused him all his troubles so far, so he was not 'going back there'.

He told me he loved reading, and I had a book in my bag which I gave to him – *The Night Circus* by Erin Morgenstern. Then Kate arrived, and I introduced them. 'You two need your time together,' Mark said, and left with a quick goodbye.

I think about him from time to time ever since, and every time I visit Spitalfields. I wonder if things got easier and he ever reconciled with his son.

My friend Flo asked me if I thought we should offer people a bed for the night, if we wanted to make a real difference, and I thought about that: how I'd be afraid to do it, nervous about all the ways it could go wrong. I thought too about how easy it is to end up sleeping rough.

After that night I investigated some of the causes of homelessness. According to the UK charity Crisis, 'Homelessness happens because there is not enough good quality, truly affordable homes available for people on the lowest incomes . . . unfair evictions, rapidly rising rents and short rental contracts make it hard for some of us to keep our home.'

Certain groups of people are more likely to experience homelessness: 'LGBTQ+ people and people of colour . . . If you are leaving prison, the care system, experiencing domestic abuse, receiving benefits or are a refugee, you are also often at greater risk from homelessness.'

Marcus Fagon, a mental health professional who works for '1625 Independent People', a young people's homelessness charity in Bristol, told me that a significant proportion of the young people he helps are care leavers: 'It can surprise people how easily someone can go homeless, until you hear the stories, then you think differently . . . so we must start by listening to the stories.'

After my chat with Mark, I thought about the effect that hearing his story had had on me: a deeper impact than reading a list of statistics, alarming as they are. According to teacher and coach Jim Kwik: 'One study conducted at the University of California, Berkeley, found that when participants listened to a speaker recount a personal story, their brain activity synchronised with the speaker. This means that the listener's brain was processing the story in a way that mirrored the speaker's brain. Researchers believe that synchronisation promotes empathy and understanding in people.' Ah, there it is again: empathy. As Ben Okri, the writer and poet, once said, 'Stories can conquer fear . . . they make the heart bigger.'

Listening to Mark's story did make my heart bigger. I thought about how easy it is to slip up. How quickly you can end up in real trouble. It was a turning point in my developing understanding of the profound importance of listening. To grow empathy by hearing each other's stories, to give our time or our attention to someone who might not receive much of either – these are among the kindest things we can do.

There was a story I was taught in my Classics lessons at school, which was introduced to us as The Beggar Test. The idea behind it is that an angel or God or some kind of higher power comes disguised as a beggar to test the hearts and compassion of the people or of a particular protagonist. The Roman poet Ovid tells the story of the gods Zeus and Hermes who came to a town disguised as ordinary peasants and began asking people for a place to sleep that night. They had been rejected by all, 'so wicked were the people of that land', when at last they came to Baucis and Philemon's simple rustic cottage. Though the couple were poor, their generosity far surpassed that of their rich neighbours, among whom the gods had found 'doors bolted and no word of kindness'.

After serving the two guests delicious and plentiful food and wine, Baucis noticed that, although she had refilled their beechwood cups many times, the pitcher was still full. Realising that her guests were in fact gods, she and her husband 'raised their hands in supplication and implored indulgence for their simple home and fare'. Zeus told them they should leave the town. He was going to destroy it and all those who had turned them away. He told Baucis and Philemon to climb the mountain with him and Hermes and not to turn back until they reached the top.

Harsh, but then the gods were harsh in those days, forever meting out awful punishments like birds pecking your liver out and rolling rocks up a hill only to have them tumble back down again, for all eternity.

Maybe this was a way of ensuring that the poor were looked after by the rich, for fear of destruction by angry gods. But there is an interesting metaphor here too: as the quote often attributed to Gandhi runs, 'How a society treats its most vulnerable is always the measure of its humanity.'

The person who is asking for money from strangers is overcoming several societal taboos. First, publicly admitting they need help (still tricky). Second, admitting they need money – and therefore admitting to their failure in acquiring it in the usual ways (working or inheriting, for example). These are cardinal sins in these times when money is how we measure the value of everything.

By mid-November it was getting colder. As I tuned in more and more to homelessness in my home city of London, I realised that stories are the currency used by the homeless to secure any kind of help. Many offer their stories, self-published on pieces of cardboard propped up next to where they are sitting. Whole lives, reduced to a few words or expressions of want and need.

They tell these stories in such a way as to demonstrate that they are worthy. There is still a prevailing Victorian notion of the 'deserving poor' – those who through no fault of their own have ended up destitute, unhoused or jobless, and are therefore deserving of help. But this also implies that there are those who choose their situation, through recklessness, poor decisions or even as a 'lifestyle choice', as it was memorably described in a series of tweets by Suella Braverman, former home secretary, in 2023. As if anyone would choose to sleep standing up in a wardrobe, or to risk the cold, hunger and violence that often accompany the experience of homelessness.

The kind choice is to help everyone in need without question, as much as we are able, and to demand that those in positions of power listen to the experts who say the solutions are to create much more social housing, to ensure that rents are fair, rental homes are decent and well maintained, and contracts take care of the needs of the tenant as well as the landlord. The right to a safe and decent home should be available to everyone, whoever they are.

I have never been street homeless, apart from one terrible night I'd rather not remember, but I have been 'insecurely housed', and not

Another Day in Paradise

so long ago either. I've had my fair share of squats, mouldy bed-and-breakfast rooms and precarious sofa-surfing. I know how disruptive and debilitating it is. How easy it is to find yourself slowly in an increasingly worse situation.

Until my year of kindness, I had very rarely spoken about my own experiences of insecure housing and homelessness. I was ashamed that I had ever been that poor and vulnerable, and I didn't want anyone's pity. I'd ended up insecurely housed by having damaging relationships with chaotic people, often those with addiction problems. And through having badly paid work, or no work despite trying my best, and by having feckless landlords, I'd lived in squats when I couldn't afford to rent and had experienced 'no fault' evictions more times than I care to mention.

But I felt that, because I hadn't been on the streets, it didn't really count. After all, I had received help: I was given a safe space in a hostel in London and then a housing association flat. I was lucky enough to be in need at a time when there was still help to be received. From this place of security I was able to rebuild my life: to get work, to support myself, to get to where I am today. But I doubt if any of these things would have happened had I not been provided with secure and affordable accommodation. I am acutely aware of the privilege of this and of how this is not available to many people today: it's what gives me a duty to speak out on this issue.

Our public spaces are full of signs telling us not to give. That year, I thought about this a lot. Many people will tell you, and they'll back it up with the very well-intentioned advice from various charities, that if you want to help then you should donate to an organisation that helps homeless people, and this is a commendable thing to do.

But I chose to give people drinks, food and money when I had it. I thought about that expression 'Beggars can't be choosers' and I thought, why not? We all get to choose, so why not afford the unhoused the same rights?

Conversations on Kindness

I know — because I speak with unhoused people every week — that someone taking time to speak with you, to care enough to offer you a cup of tea or a sandwich, is priceless. Simply being treated with compassion and empathy, one to one, as a human being worthy of care and attention, is essential. I understand the reluctance to give actual cash (although I still do this sometimes too) — there's a worry that you would be helping someone hurt themselves if they have addiction problems. But there is no harm in a conversation, or an offer of a bottle of water, a snack. What you are giving, when you give someone personal attention in this way, is hope.

On Day 309 of my year, I saw a homeless man take his trainers off outside St Paul's Church in the jewellery quarter in Birmingham. His feet were bleeding. Here is our conversation:

Me: Hello. I know this is a bit odd, but do you want my socks? They're clean and I've just had a shower, honest.
Him: Yes, please.
Me: When I saw you, I thought to myself, I hate wearing trainers without socks.
Him: So do I. Feet are hard.

We had a chat about how cold it was, and then we went our separate ways. When I walked back past the door of the church, I saw a sign saying:

PLEASE DO NOT ENCOURAGE BEGGARS

Looking back, I wished I had crossed the 'not' out on that sign. Surely, we do need to encourage anyone who is so vulnerable and poor that they can't afford socks and that makes their feet bleed. We need to encourage them by being kind.

Another Day in Paradise

These days we don't carry cash much anymore — Covid put paid to that. But we are carrying around so much anguish and worry, it is easy and entirely understandable to put our heads down and rush by. I'm not asking you to feel guilty. But I am saying, when you are able, take every opportunity to ask people experiencing homelessness how they are.

As Mark said to me that day in Spitalfields as we spoke about his daily experiences of life on the street, 'Even when people say "I haven't got anything, I am sorry", it is better, because they have seen me.'

So, please, if you have money, you could buy someone a cup of tea. If you have time, you could have a quick chat. If you have strength, just a smile, and if you have none of those to offer, that is okay — you need all of those things more and that is important too.

But perhaps we need to find out *why* are there so many unhoused and vulnerable people on the streets. Do we have to just accept that there will always be rich and poor, and that a degree of homelessness is inevitable?

To help me find the answers to these questions, I spoke with the Labour economist Professor Lord Layard, who co-founded the charity Action for Happiness and who has worked for most of his life on how to reduce unemployment and inequality.

Happiness over Profit
with Professor Lord Layard

During my first year of carrying out daily acts of kindness, I met and spoke with a lot of people experiencing homelessness. Some of them told me that they were treated kindly and others talked about how they felt judged, or even blamed, for the position that they found themselves in. If our current definition of success is only about money and wealth, do you believe that is why unhoused people, or the poor, or other disadvantaged people, are sometimes treated badly?

Well, I think there are two things there. First is the general point: you should be kind to everybody, whether homeless or not. Secondly what matters in society is what goals you think people should have. When I discovered that economics was really designed as a system for thinking about how you organise society in the way that produces the most happiness, and that was the motivation for the development of economics, well I thought that was terrific! So, if the goal of individual people, and of society in general, is producing the most happiness, not the most profit, well then, that changes everything.

I wonder if you could speak about the idea which emerged in the eighteenth century, expressed by Jeremy Bentham and others, that you should judge how a country is doing by how happy the people are?

Yes, there were quite a lot of figures in the eighteenth century who had the same wonderful idea that the right thing to do is to try to create the most happiness you can in the world. And this would apply to governments, and a law would only be justified if it could be shown to increase the happiness of the population. I just thought this was such a tremendously inspiring idea for individual action, but also such a sensible idea when you're talking about public policy.

And how and why did this idea change?

It got undermined in the twentieth century by psychologists who said that you couldn't know anything about what was going on inside anybody else: the only thing you could do was to observe their behaviour. And so you got this terrible period dominated by behaviourists that completely undermined the idea that you should judge your actions by how they affected other people's happiness, or that public policy could be based on

Another Day in Paradise

how it would be likely to affect the happiness of the population. Into this void rushed the idea that the GDP was a good measure of the success of the country.[1] GDP was never invented for the purpose of measuring a country's welfare. The science of happiness[2] has been able to develop an alternative measure of wellbeing, and you could then base public policy on what seems to be most important — making people happy and preventing them being miserable.

If you contrast the goal of promoting the most happiness you can in people you can affect, to the goal of being successful *compared* with other people — for example having better grades at school, having a better job, having a bigger income — well, logic dictates that in the second case there's no way in which the amount of success in society can ever increase, because for every person who does relatively well, somebody else has to do relatively badly.

So, we've got to have objectives which are positive, where people are getting their happiness from helping other people rather than from doing better than other people. There are two unhelpful ideas in our culture: one is the idea that you should be pursuing personal success, and the other is that people get their just deserts. We absolutely must get away from thinking that it is somebody who's struggling who is to blame, because they brought it on themselves, didn't they? It is a terrible

---

[1] A brief reminder: GDP stands for gross domestic product. It is a monetary measure of the market value of all the final goods and services produced in a specific time period by a country or countries. It's most often used by governments of a single country to measure its economic health.

[2] The science of happiness is the scientific study of 'what makes happy people happy' and was arguably launched by Mihaly Csikszentmihalyi in the late 1980s. The concept is now picking up speed, with scientists from around the globe exploring the neuroscience of happiness as well as the psychology of wellbeing. The measurement of happiness has consequently become a major focus of the new science, with many scales presently being used, depending on how 'happiness' is defined.

attitude. You see this obviously in attitudes towards the poor, the unemployed, the unhoused and so on.

Yes, and I can see this gap between harsh or unhelpful government policy and how people are, which is compassionate and helpful to each other for the most part. How can we match up the compassion of ordinary people with government policy? Do we simply write to our MPs? Make sure we vote for a more compassionate party? Is it simple as that?

Well, the good news is that we're part of a movement which is trying to make governments adopt people's wellbeing as their objective. This has been sometimes called 'beyond GDP', but it's become focused on the word 'wellbeing', which policymakers do seem to find a reasonably acceptable word. And you've got, for example, both the European Union and the Organisation for Economic Co-operation and Development, which are the rich nations, saying to their members, 'Please, put people's wellbeing at the centre of decision-making.' But we need to move from a point where people are saying this, to where they're actually doing it. There are a few countries which have done some things explicitly with that philosophy in mind. And these are the countries that belong to what's called the Wellbeing Economy Governments alliance, which includes New Zealand, Finland, Iceland, Canada, Scotland and Wales. They have at least recognised that it's very important that we get wellbeing and happiness adopted as the explicit goal.

As Thomas Jefferson said, 'The only legitimate objective of government is the happiness of the people.' So we've really got to get that accepted. And then the people who make the decisions, which is largely the civil servants in the Treasury departments around the world, have them analyse policies in terms of their impact on wellbeing. This is what I have spent a lot of time on, to show how that can be done, and to persuade people to do it. It's an incredibly important change that we're trying to bring about, to get away from the macho approach to policymaking. It is essential that we get governments to care, in particular about the wellbeing of the least fortunate. We've got evidence of what are the main causes of misery in the population – and they are poor mental health, physical pain, destructive relationships and poverty. It's important to get away from the idea that poverty is the sole cause of misery, as it isn't, but it is widely believed to be so in some political circles.

Could you tell me about Action for Happiness and the cornerstone of its work? And about how, for you, kindness and happiness are connected?

Well, there are two ways. Obviously, if you're kind, that's nicer for other people, and that's the main reason. But there's also the side effect for yourself, which is that one of the best ways to make you feel better is to make other people feel better, to do something which is useful to other people. Which has got many aspects to it. One is simply the intrinsic quiet pleasure of doing the right thing. The other, of course, is not so lofty. It's nice, of course, that people appreciate what you're doing. But I've always been very struck by these experiments in neuroscience where we see the standard reward centres in our brains light up when we are nice to someone. One should never say that you should be kind because you will benefit. But it is a fact nonetheless that in general kind people do become a lot happier in comparison to people who do not focus on kindness. So the motto of Action for Happiness is 'Happier and Kinder, Together'.

Are you confident about the innate goodness and kindness of human beings? And if you are, why?

In general, I find that if you treat people well, they respond well. I believe that there is in everybody a mixture of unselfish goodness and selfishness, and the main task of what you might call the value system of a community is to push people to support the unselfish part. To me, that's incredibly important. And I think that that's why we hate this ultra-competitive macho culture, that is probably the dominant culture now, because it's constantly behaving as if the only element in the human being that can be relied on for motivation is the selfish part. Which is simply not true.

Given the challenges that we are all facing now, do you feel optimistic about the future?

I am optimistic about the future. I mean, in most parts of the world we are living in about the best time that has existed for humanity. So, if we have come this far, we can go further. We launched last year what we call a 'World Wellbeing Movement', which is a movement to pressure governments and businesses to put wellbeing at the top of their priorities. Hopefully the world will hear a lot more from that movement in the future.

I want to say that I think that the job you decide to do is one of the most important decisions you make in terms of your contribution to the happiness of the world. Because, of course, this includes your own happiness: you're not going to do much good if you're just making yourself miserable. And I think the idea that you should treat people who are in front of you with kindness is essential. I've always been struck with Tolstoy's remark: the most important person in the world is the person in front of you, so treat that that person with compassion. That's incredibly important.

From Richard I learned that we must not assume that the state we're in is the state we will always be in. That there have been better ideas in the past which we can learn from. That there are radical and better ideas now, such as those he shared with me. We must find the courage to support those who are trying to make real change happen, change that will result in a fairer, kinder and more equitable world. And to be kind when we have the opportunity in the place and moment we are in.

Another Day in Paradise

Being brave enough to face the suffering in the world and to keep strong and positive requires a balancing act I was beginning to get the hang of. But when I found myself faltering, I remembered the words of another man I met, also called Mark, who was sitting on his blanket outside the Apollo Theatre on Shaftesbury Avenue one day. We got chatting, and I stayed with him for a while and bought him a sandwich and a cup of tea. He told me something that has always stayed with me: that he 'tries to say yes to every opportunity, tries to always stay cheerful and tries to think the best of people'.

I promised myself there and then to remember him, and I recommitted to taking time to speak with and listen to people who were experiencing homelessness, as they are so often the person right in front of us.

5. DECEMBER

I Gotta Have Faith

Five acts of kindness this month:

Day 106: While in Portsmouth with work, I stayed in a hotel on the road I lived on when I was seventeen. I left a note and a present outside the front door of the house explaining who I was and why I was leaving it.

Day 110: I left a small gift in the self-help section of Canada Water library.

Day 114: I gave my friend a handmade card with a kind message inside to deliver randomly to someone at a party. I got this message back from the recipient: 'This made me so happy! . . . thank you Bernadette x.' Nice.

Day 127: I delivered goodies to a local arts centre for their Christmas Day seniors' party. Loads of friends contributed cakes, snacks and mince pies

Day 129: I met an Aussie barman at the Mayflower pub in Bermondsey and gave him a Christmas card after finding out he was a long way from home. I saw him again in the new year. 'I had a shit Christmas because I had no family here, so thanks so much for the card, I loved it,' he said.

I love December and the run-up to Christmas. It's easy to feel cynical about it, to see it as a festival of shopping, and it is very hard if you have little money when there is so much pressure to buy all the shiny things, especially if you have children. I know that my mum often struggled at Christmas, and it is not a bundle of joy for everyone. If you live alone, or you don't have much spare cash, or you're grieving, or you are someone for whom social gatherings can be uncomfortable, then Christmas can be tough. But still I love that the windows are twinkly with fairy lights, and all the people dressed as Santa in badly fitting fake white beards, and that as a storyteller I spend a lot of this month hanging out with people dressed as elves, in grottos filled with fake snow. It's one of the times of year strangers are more comfortable with speaking with each other, even if just to say, 'Merry Christmas' (and it's possibly the only time of year 'merry' gets said at all). We're encouraged, via advertisements and social media posts, to think more about others who may be 'less fortunate'. It's a month with a sparkle of kindness threaded through it like tinsel.

As many people do, I have my own traditions at this time of year. I always watch *A Christmas Carol* and it never, ever fails to cheer me up. In case you're not familiar with it, I'll summarise Charles Dickens' classic story, for you. Ebenezer Scrooge, a miser and mean-spirited curmudgeon, learns the error of his ways when he is visited on Christmas Eve by the ghosts of Christmas past, present and future. With dismay he witnesses his mistakes and missteps, and what his future holds if he carries on like this. But he gets a chance to redeem himself, and he seizes that opportunity with glee. His life is greatly improved at the end of the story by his newfound generosity and kindness. He becomes a good uncle, employer and friend, and resolves to 'honour Christmas in my heart, and try to keep it all the year'.

As Scrooge discovered, the magic of Christmas is kindness. And the statistics agree with us here. According to the thinktank CGAP, 'There is a 5 per cent increase in the numbers of people giving at Christmas.' Likewise, a winter report from Enthuse, a platform for digital fundraising, found that 42 per cent of people are more likely to donate to charity during the festive season. A survey carried out via OnePoll by Costa Coffee in 2021 found that of the 2,000 people studied, four out of five were actively planning to go out of their way to be kinder during the festive period, with ideas such as donating to foodbanks, buying vulnerable community members gifts and making sure that anyone who was

I Gotta Have Faith

feeling lonely had company. You could say that being kind is one of our Christmas traditions.

But in our multi-cultural, multi-faith society, Christmas isn't the only winter festival – there are loads of others around this time of year. I have been introduced to some of these by friends, colleagues and neighbours over the years, such as Hanukkah (the Hebrew 'festival of lights' that usually takes place in late November or December), the Hindu Diwali (October/November, celebrating 'victory of light over darkness, good over evil, knowledge over ignorance') and Yule (the Pagan festival celebrating the 'return of the light' after the Winter Solstice, around 21 December). Kindness lies at the heart of all these religious holidays.

With this in mind, I began to consider faith: my own faith in people and myself, our faith in each other, and the broader idea of faith and how it fits with kindness. What 'to have faith' even means . . .

In a previous chapter, I told the story of when I had given the 'Sad Lady in Boots' a bunch of flowers and saw her cry. But the sadness didn't end there that day. After I said goodbye to her, as I was walking home, I saw a woman with a walking stick struggling up the very steep stairs to her front door. I asked her if she needed any help.

'You're very kind, but no, thanks,' she said. 'I'm okay, just sometimes I'm in a lot of pain, and today is very hard.' Her eyes filled with tears, and as she carried on up the stairs I made a mental note of the number of her house, muttering to myself as I walked home, so that I would remember to drop her off a card or a small gift later.

I imagined what it must be like to be in constant pain, to have to negotiate stairs every day when it is so difficult to walk. I thought about how some parts of our cities are still not easy for anyone with mobility issues, or in a wheelchair. Or with a buggy. Or for children. A lot has improved, of course, but there are still challenges for some people, and I had not always been fully aware of them, until then.

Much later on the same day, I was at the bus stop, on my way to a night out in nearby Greenwich, when I saw a young man sitting there with his head in his hands. I thought I should check in and see if he was okay, so I did.

Barely lifting his head he said, 'Some people aren't meant for love.' I was shocked. 'What do you mean? You are . . . A nice person like you,' I said, cringing immediately at how stupid and ineffectual my words sounded. But his honesty had taken me by surprise.

'No, no, some people aren't meant for love,' he repeated, and started to sob.

The bus came and we both got on. I watched him out of the corner of my eye – he was crying, he might have been a little bit drunk. I felt deflated. All these things had happened in one day. It was quite overwhelming. *It seems like everyone in Deptford is crying*, I thought to myself. Maybe my kindly intentions had even made these people feel worse. I certainly hadn't been able to cheer any of them up in any obvious way.

This challenged me: could this mean that kindness was not enough, that it *couldn't* change the world, that it didn't have any real power? Or was it just that in practising my daily acts of kindness I had become more aware of those around me? And that this is wonderful and magical, but painful too. You see and feel all the sadness in the world, the loneliness and the suffering, as well as the joy.

So the next morning, to cheer myself up, I decided to create something to leave for other people. I chose the noticeboard of St Paul's Church, which is halfway down Deptford High Street and can easily be seen by anyone out and about in the market or the shops. I wanted to make something beautiful that might put a smile on people's faces. A small thing that I could put my faith in. I got my craft kit out. I really went to town: I used stickers, paints, washi tape, and cut up old magazines to create a collage for an A3-sized poster which said, 'Hope you have a nice day – be kind to yourself. P.S. Can kindness change the world? What do you think?'

I Gotta Have Faith

It was pretty and jolly and, I hoped to myself, the very least it would do is put a smile on a few faces, and make people think.

It was the first time in a very long time I had been anywhere near a church. My family weren't churchgoers, my grandad was most definitely an atheist, my nana a Christian but not a churchgoing one. My mum always used to say she wasn't Christian, but she did 'believe in something'. I chose to go to Sunday School because there were free jelly tots and colouring-in books. But my greatest introduction to Jesus came from my schoolteacher Mrs Hibdidge, who was an amazing storyteller. She was Greek, with a distinct accent which I had never heard before and was fascinated by, and she smelled of strong coffee, which was interesting too, as everyone I knew drank tea. And she had perfect hair. There was a lot to love about her.

Mrs Hibdidge told us her version of stories from the Bible. She held a book open, but she did not appear to read from it — it was as if the stories just poured from her. As she told it, Jesus came across as this really kind, really cool, animal-loving, magician type who hosted very large, very successful social events. He was unfailingly nice to children and usually spoke softly. Bad people were made good just by attending his amazing parties. This was my impression of the life of Jesus from Mrs Hibdidge, and I loved him so much. Like me, he adored animals; like me, he wanted everyone to be nice; like me, he loved being outside. On the wall of our classroom were some posters with quotes from the Sermon on the Mount which said, 'Blessed are the peacemakers, for they will be called children of God.' I loved that too.

At Christmas, Mrs Hibdidge would help us decorate oranges with cloves and ribbons to take to church so it smelled gorgeous, and there were candles and singing. At school I got to play a donkey in the nativity, gently clopping coconut shells together and looking a bit melancholy — perhaps my greatest role ever. Looking back, I liked the awe of the sermons, the beauty of the church and the poetry of the verses, as well as the promise in Mrs Hibdidge's stories that goodness prevailed.

But by the time I reached eleven, I was becoming quite disappointed and disillusioned by religion. There seemed to be a general undercurrent of disapproval of most things. The vicar told me animals didn't have souls, which seemed ludicrous. There were only men in charge, as far as I could tell, and the more grown-up services were joyless and boring. When we moved again, I stopped going. But secretly and deep down I missed it. I missed kind Jesus, the one I thought I'd got to know quite well. When I got to teenagerhood, most of my friends were passionately atheist to the extent that I would not have dared to mention that I once went to church and actually enjoyed it. I had always had queer friends and it did feel like Church God was mean to gay people, which seemed really unfair and most unlike Mrs Hibdidge's version of kind Jesus, who liked everyone, and I felt sure would give anyone a fish sandwich.

As I put my sign on the church noticeboard on Deptford High Street that day, I saw other notices: little homemade flyers for coffee mornings or 'knit and natter'. They seemed like sweet invitations for people to meet each other in their community, in a beautiful space that didn't cost anything to enter.

The next day on London Bridge I saw a van where people were dispensing soup and rolls to homeless people, and I got chatting to them and they told me they came from a local mosque. I saw the Sikh community giving away free food to anyone who needed it in Leicester Square. I saw a vicar take sleeping bags and blankets down to the South Bank for the rough sleepers. On Facebook there were appeals from intergenerational choirs of elders and children from all kinds of faith groups raising funds for charities.

I began to notice how many of the examples of kindness I was seeing were linked to religion. I have friends of all faiths, but I realised I'd never really spoken to any of them about how their faith had affected them in terms of how they think about the practice of kindness.

I Gotta Have Faith

Shortly afterwards, my friend James Yarker emailed me a picture of Christchurch in Summerfield, Birmingham. The vicar was Peter Sainsbury. The church had hosted a talk about kindness and there had been a bit in the service about what I'd been doing. I was really chuffed. How unlikely it seemed that a huge picture of me would appear on the wall of a church in Birmingham — how strange and wonderful my life had become. This all seemed like a great opportunity to go and speak to this vicar Pete and see what he had to say about religion and kindness. He told me about an initiative the church in Birmingham had undertaken just after that original talk, called Places of Welcome, where anybody could come and get tea, coffee, croissants, toast and a sense of welcome inside the church. There wasn't a missionary angle to this — it was just a way of being practically kind to the wider community. One quote he told me stayed with me, from William Booth, founder of the Salvation Army: 'You cannot warm the hearts of people with God's love if they have an empty stomach and cold feet.'

Pete left Birmingham in 2020, and is now in a church in Marlborough, Wiltshire. After all these years, I was interested to return to the big questions we touched on when we first met, to see what has changed and what may have stayed the same.

God Is Love
with Pete Sainsbury

I was wondering if your understanding of Christianity having kindness at the heart of its teachings came from a particular part of the Bible? Or did it come from a particular practice or belief?

It came from the example of others. I grew up in a churchgoing home, but it wasn't a place where religious belief was that important. When I was about twelve, I began to have questions, and a couple of years later

Conversations on Kindness

I came across people at school, older than me, who called themselves Born Again Christians. They seemed quite nice, and not too weird! So, I joined their meetings, and they were prepared to take fourteen-year-old me seriously. I was just soaking it all in, and they gave me time. I went on some Christian camps, and the leaders would give me time too. They would take my questions seriously, and they would want to answer them. So, I think for me there was a lot about the kindness of giving me time and people's interest in my life. And I was loved by those Christian leaders.

So it sounds like you found a strong sense of belonging with them?

Yes, I found my people, really. I was loved, and I think if you know you are loved you don't have a problem loving others. And when people are showing you great kindness it's not difficult to be kind.

When we spoke before, I asked you if you felt that kindness is at the heart of all the world's religions, and you said yes. Do you still think that?

I do. I think that the essence of expected behaviour in the world's religions is a kind of 'treat others as you'd like to be treated yourself'. For example, there is a very hospitable tradition in Islam, and in all the major world faiths. I think kindness is very important to all of them.

Given that there is a wide variety of faiths and belief systems in our world, how can we best be kind to each other and find a way of coexisting peacefully, with these different beliefs?

I think we've got to respect each other's rights to hold specific convictions with which we may strongly disagree. Good disagreement has become very difficult in our culture. So I think learning how to disagree well is an important part of kindness.

It reminds me again of the importance of active listening.

I Gotta Have Faith

Yes, active listening is so important for people of different views. There was a great initiative in Birmingham which focused on this, called The Feast. It aimed to bring young people of different faiths and cultural backgrounds together, to learn about each other's traditions, to eat and spend time together, to build friendships. By talking and listening they learn about the similarities and differences that exist between different faiths.

It seems to me that religious communities provide so many important and powerful things: community, belonging, purpose and I guess it all leads back to love, to giving and receiving love.

Yes, I think that all Christians will agree that God is love, and kindness, of course, flows from that. And kindness is active. If we live kindly as well as being kindly intentioned, there is something obviously powerful about that.

One thing Pete told me was that 'all the world major religions have kindness at the heart of their teachings'. So I investigated it a little. I had a lot of conversations with friends, and the broad-stroke conclusion I came to (thank you to all for your patience!) from chatting with Bharti about Hinduism, Navdeep about Sikhism, Helena about Judaism, Asif about Islam and Annie about Buddhism – to name but a very few of the people I have pestered – is yes, kindness matters to all of them. I'd also like to add here that I have many friends who identify as atheists, humanists and agnostics, all of whom also cite kindness as an important guiding principle and value system. In the brilliant Claudia Hammond's book *The Keys to Kindness*, I found this, too: 'Value systems are . . . more important than religion. Those who say they value benevolence and universalism are kinder on average than those who value achievement and power.' So it seems this is true: no matter what your religion, or if you have one at all, if you value benevolence, you will be kinder.

It was when I came across the comforting idea of 'The Golden Rule' that I felt like I'd found the place and space where all religions and value systems could meet in agreement. The Golden Rule is an idea which comes from Christianity (from the Gospel of Matthew) which could be summed up as 'Treat others as you would have them treat you.' Perhaps the recent update or the New Golden Rule is even more compassionate: 'Treat others as they would like to be treated.'

As Rumi, the thirteenth-century Sufi mystic and poet, wrote:

Out beyond ideas of wrongdoing and rightdoing there is a field.
I'll meet you there.
When the soul lies down in that grass
the world is too full to talk about.

Maybe kindness is that field. A place of being with each other, with all our differences and ideas, with our joys and challenges, where we can agree on this: to treat one another kindly.

I can see that to be part of a tradition, be it Christian, Muslim, Hindu, Sikh or whatever, can give you a lot: a sense of belonging, purpose, community and support. I can see so much good being done by faith groups all over the world. But also, it must be said, great harm, violence and suffering are carried out in the name of religion. The solution is not simple. We must find the courage to ask ourselves what we can do, even in the face of ongoing horrific conflict and war. Perhaps a kind thing to do would be to learn about each other's ideas, beliefs and philosophies. To speak to friends and neighbours, colleagues and family members about their beliefs, religious and non-religious – ones you agree with and ones you may not. To listen. To be curious. And to celebrate the golden thread of kindness that weaves through them all.

And so, I was returned to faith. Not to the Christianity I had been drawn to as a child, but to a faith in the kindness, strength and wisdom

I Gotta Have Faith

of human beings, and in the vast beauty, mystery and wonder of the whole universe. I realised that I do believe in God, or a Higher Power, or 'something', as my mum said. Sometimes I squirm away from those words 'God' and 'faith', but here I'd like to reclaim them.

I regained the faith I had had as a child that by everyday small actions I could effect real, lasting and positive change in the world and in myself; that I could make myself happier, my life more interesting, and put a smile on the face of at least one person a day. I had faith that this could ripple out – something I came to call the magic of kindness. A transformative alchemical process whereby a simple act of kindness can transform a mood, a day, even perhaps a life, as it had done for me.

My god is love, as expressed by kind acts, as demonstrated by the vast beauty and interconnectedness of the earth and all her inhabitants. By the wisdom and grace of the more than human, too. And it's bound together with the scientific knowledge 'that energy can neither be created nor destroyed – only converted from one form of energy to another'. And with the knowledge that when I die my body will decompose and I will break down and become part of the natural world forever, as these beautiful words from the painter Edvard Munch express: 'From my rotting body, flowers shall grow and I am in them, and that is eternity.'

That December, a lot transformed for me.

Let me take you back to the church noticeboard for a moment. When I walked back past it later that day, I saw that, underneath my question, 'Can kindness change the world?', someone had written YES, in capital letters. It meant a lot, to feel that 'YES' in my heart.

And I thought again about Scrooge, and what it might look like 'to keep Christmas all year around'. Maybe it would look like striving to take care of those who have less than us, to put connection and experience above monetary profit, to aim to be remembered for kindness rather than how important or rich we were in life. It seems like a good lesson.

6. JANUARY

The Bad News Blues

Five acts of kindness this month:

Day 140: I put a lottery ticket in a golden envelope and delivered it to a house on my street.

Day 146: I was in Deptford Train Carriage Café decorating a jar of sweets to give to someone and trying to order a flat white. The waitress saw what I was doing (tying a ribbon round a piece of gingham, all fingers and thumbs) and she said, 'I love that.' So, she got it.

Day 149: I got an amazing email from the person who was 11 January's recipient of a box of kindness through the post. 'As I opened the box and looked in lovingly at the gifts, my face felt like a big beam of smiles, and then I started to sob tears of joy. It really was a wonderful moment – thank you so much, Bernadette – what a wonderful thing you are doing and what fun you must have putting all these things together, making bits and pieces and making the cards too, loved the glitter and the little box and the gifts are perfect.'

Day 151: Via Twitter from a stranger: 'I was wondering if I could get some little bit of kindness in the post for my birthday. It's next Wednesday, 18 January, but I feel a bit low because it's so close to my late husband's birthday, that was on 16 January. He'd be forty if he hadn't died a year and a half ago. Please surprise me, I love surprises!' I sent her a card and gift through the post.

Day 162: I left a homemade chocolate in a silver box outside my neighbour's house. It's safe to say that if you lived within a five-mile radius of my house, you got a surprise on your doorstep during that year.

I love that it's quieter at this time of year. I enjoy seeing the winter bones of the trees in the parks. I like that you're allowed to stay in and wear big cardigans. It's a good time of year for an introvert. You can pause. So long as you haven't sworn to long-distance running every day from 1 January, that is.

Of course, January is traditionally a time of new beginnings in the Western world. It's named after Janus, the Roman god of beginnings and transitions — and of doors — so this month can be perceived as offering us access to different ways of thinking, perceiving or living.

It's a time when many of us make those resolutions to recommit to going to the gym, or learning a new language, or redecorating our homes. It's also a bit of a celebration hangover. Whether you celebrate Christmas or drink alcohol or not, the general vibe is a subdued tightening of belts. January can feel serious, and a little dour, given that it's traditionally focused on giving things up, on doing things less. It *can* feel a little self-punishing.

But it was in the relative post-party quiet of January 2012 that I had the opportunity to take a breath and reflect on my experience so far. For the first time I began to question whether I should be sharing these stories of my year of kindness publicly. Was it being seen as showing off? That wasn't my intention. It was a way of keeping a diary and imposing some order on my quest. I always asked the strangers I interacted with if I could take a picture of them and let them know I was sharing this on social media. I paid attention to the reactions I got online (overwhelmingly positive) and in person (the same). The responses helped me feel part of a community, gave me encouragement and feedback, and held me to account, in a friendly way.

Gleb Tsipursky from Giving What We Can, an organisation that actively encourages people to talk about their giving, points out that 'giving publicly helps create a social norm by inspiring others'.

The Bad News Blues

Giving What We Can also cites research that shows that, since we tend to evaluate ourselves based on what our peers think of us – both online and in person – we tend to 'model behaviours that will cause others to have positive opinions about us.' As they say, 'Ideas cannot spread unless we share them.'

The term 'social proof' was coined in 1984 by psychologist Robert Cialdini in his book *Influence – The Psychology of Persuasion*. At its simplest, social proof is about the psychological and social phenomenon of people copying the behaviour of others. In other words: we are more likely to do things if we see others doing them. And that's exactly what began to happen.

People were telling me how much my stories had cheered them up. I received many messages from people saying they had joined in by doing acts of kindness themselves. I was hugely encouraged, and I still think of this on the days when social media feels like a quagmire of misery and bickering: good things can and are shared in those spaces too.

These responses were the first direct evidence I had of the 'ripple effect' of kindness – the power of a single act to encourage others (the recipient of the act as well as those who witnessed it) to be kind themselves, potentially inspiring multiple subsequent acts of kindness, ad infinitum . . . Was this ripple effect *how* kindness could change the world? Perhaps . . .

This month I also noticed how I felt when I read a funny or heartwarming story on social media, in contrast to how I felt when I read a story about anger or violence or injustice. I began to pay close attention to the news and the way it is reported.

I started to ask myself why all the news was focused on the suffering and misery in the world; I began to notice how little reporting seemed to ask why things were as they were. Where was the news about how often people are kind to each other, the reports about how much people care for each other and the world? I get it – 'Man helps another man carry a heavy suitcase up stairs in King's Cross Station, both men feel mildly encouraged by the interaction' – it's not much of a headline. But still, I couldn't see the need for so much bad news, relentlessly.

I started casting my eye over the displays in newsagents' shop windows, noticing the headlines as I scrolled through the social media feeds on my phone. Doom scrolling, yes, but with a purpose. I was thinking, *Most people are kind, they really are, but you'd never believe that if all you did was watch the news all day. Instead, all you'd see would be a world full of terrible people and terrible things and nothing else. Why is that?*

Inspired by these dreadful headlines, I put together a poem – I called it 'The Bad News Blues' – as a fun way to try to work out why exactly it is so easy for us to think the absolute worst of each other, to believe – in the words of the mighty Nick Cave – 'people ain't no good.'

The Bad News (12-Bar) Blues
Be afraid of the future because it's looking grim
And do not trust experts, they think we're all dim
Be afraid of people because people are bad
And don't trust anyone, they're all stupid or mad
Be afraid of foreigners and stick to your own
And if the doorbell rings when you're home alone
It's probably a scammer or a weirdo or worse
Or a wild-eyed chugger who will grab for your purse
Be afraid of immigrants arriving at sea
Even the children can't be trusted, if you ask me
They'll be taking our houses and stealing our jobs
But they're lazy and feckless, they're all big fat slobs
Be afraid of the poor as they scrounge off the state
Buying TVs and scratch cards and staying up late

The Bad News Blues

And single mums and their dozens of kids
And that lonely old man, you don't know what he did

Be afraid of the hoodie on his own in the park
He might clobber you on the head once it's turned into dark
And you cannot trust no one and nobody cares
And don't go out at night, you just don't dare

And it's not like the old days we should bring back hanging
And what's that? I can hear – a terrible banging
It's someone at the door and they say they want sugar
I wish this were America so I could shoot the bugger
Be afraid of women having brains and not just boobs
Be afraid of developing unsightly moobs
Be afraid to laugh, be afraid to cry
Be afraid to live before you die
And dogs and dog owners and child-eating foxes
And things you must sign for delivered in boxes
Be afraid of peanuts (but they can kill you, it's true)
Be afraid of cancer and vaccines and flu
And sea levels rising and population growth
And carbon emissions and marmite on toast
And midges and mozzies in countryside fields
And microwaved horses in beef ready meals
Be afraid.

Yes, this seems to be the intended message. 'Be afraid. There are so many situations and people of which to be scared.'

    We do need fear to protect us from dangers – it can serve a useful purpose – but often it seems we are being actively encouraged by the mainstream media to be particularly afraid of certain kinds of 'others':

poor people, young people, people who live on council estates or who wear hoodies. But what if you find yourself included in that list of 'others' who must be feared? The people who were being demonised were people like me and my friends and the people I live next door to, so it made me angry and frustrated.

A much greater diversity in newsrooms might be a way of balancing out this kind of reporting. Newsrooms and newspapers are still mostly owned and run by a narrow range of people. In fact, according to a Pew Research Center analysis in 2016, only 23 per cent of newsroom employees were global majority – female and non-binary, queer, working class, disabled – and 61 per cent of newsroom employees were men. If there were more global majority voices in the media, surely this would make for a more balanced perspective?

It seems sensible that a diversity of views and perspectives would help the reporting of complex matters. Of course, it wouldn't automatically mean that more positive stories would be broadcast or published, or that kindness would be more highly valued by news agencies, but it seems fairer and kinder to accommodate and platform a wider range of voices with a wider variety of experiences. I wondered what potential there might be in this changing media landscape to 'change the news for good'?

To discuss this, I returned to my friend and colleague Kamilah McInnis (with whom I discussed the language of flowers in Chapter 2) and here we are talking about positive news, fake news and the importance of different perspectives.

The Bad News Blues

Telling a Different Story
with Kamilah McInnis

I'm aware that we have evolved a 'negativity bias', to protect ourselves and our communities, so we notice and remember things that might harm us. It does make sense, but I feel like too much bad and negative news can also cause us harm.

I do think in recent years that there has been this kind of growing movement of more positive news organisations and people paying attention to happier news. For instance, the BBC World Service has a podcast called *People Fixing the World*, which covers brilliant solutions to the world's problems. We do need to report on the world's challenges because people need to know what's going on. But I think it's about getting the balance right. I really want to do more research into the benefits of uplifting and inspiring news, so that I can also go to news organisations and feed back on the appetite for these kind of stories.

I think this idea that the negative stories are intellectually superior, that maybe needs to be challenged as well. And perhaps when we share negative stories, we should present solutions or invitations to help where possible.

Actually, that's a hard one, because it can be quite taxing, trying to find solutions when sometimes there just aren't any. I've spoken to other journalists about this, and some of them have said that, Kamilah, it's not on you to have to present solutions. That's not your job. You're just supposed to report.

So how might someone support you and other journalists who are focusing on compassionate, kind journalism?

That really is a tricky one. Something that I do notice on social media is a lot of people sharing and commenting on things before actually reading the article, just seeing a headline, and then becoming enraged or misinterpreting it. So I guess, for starters, read the article before jumping to conclusions.

So, if you see a story that looks unbelievable, and is backed up by a TikTok 'journalist' that isn't actually a journalist, I'd say please refrain from just sharing it, because that adds fuel to the fire. So yes, it's reading the articles thoroughly, trying not to share fake news. I'll give you an example. A story went around on social media about the BBC news presenter Clive Myrie, which said that he was targeted and beaten up by Ukrainian racist thugs while reporting on the war, and that the BBC was covering it up. That travelled around the black community and I received many Whatsapp messages about it. And I spent my time replying to people saying, this isn't true, this isn't true, this isn't true. And I just wish that people would have thought before sharing it and read into it, and thought, hold on: Whose source is this? Where did this story originate from? How plausible is this? Those are the two things that I would say are my takeaway.

I know that I can feel myself doing it, when I read something and it's like a flashpoint, I experience this immediate and fierce emotional reaction. So it seems like a good idea to pause and reflect before you react

My conversation with Kamilah gave me a lot of hope: that the range of voices across the media is becoming more diverse, that the appetite for solutions-driven and positive stories is growing.

Sarah Browning runs a wellbeing programme called Time for Kindness, which focuses on the power of sharing stories of kindness on social media. I had a catch-up with Sarah to hear her thoughts about this kind of reporting, which is delivered not by professional journalists but by us – ordinary people using the available tools we have, including social media, for the good.

The Bad News Blues

It's Time for Stories about Kindness
with Sarah Browning

Could you share a little about how the brilliant Time for Kindness began?

It came about in late 2020, when I was thinking, *What on earth is going on? Who am I? What am I doing?* That sort of thing! I'm a communications consultant by profession, and I've always specialised in working with charities and other non-profit organisations, and I understood that my clients had a vision of a better world. And at that point in time, I asked myself, yes, but what does 'a better world' mean? And then I thought, it means kindness, that's what is important to me. And I think there is lots of kindness in the world already, but we just don't talk about it enough yet. So it came from the desire to rebalance that narrative. Having thought that, I thought, okay, so what can I do about it? And how can I help to communicate these stories of kindness that are happening? So it was all about real stories, in the real world, examples of kindness that are going on, and that's where I started. What I discovered once I started sharing those stories was that I'm not the only one who believes in the power of them. There were many people saying, 'Oh, that's great! I love it! And I really enjoy what you're doing.' And so, then it's grown from there. But that's where it started.

And how did you begin to gather the stories?

Well, my then thirteen-year-old daughter taught me how to use Instagram, and I had heard that Instagram has a more positive vibe generally than other platforms, because it's quite visual and quite story-led, and so on. So I set up the account with my daughter, who came up with the name 'Time for Kindness' as well. That first year it was a lot of stories that I spotted and examples I saw, and friends and family giving me their examples and sharing their stories, and then it's grown. Now we get stories from lots of other places as well.

I run workshops and people do tell me that, once you start noticing, you find kindness everywhere, and I've always been keen to point that out. This is not about saying the bad stuff isn't happening, or let's ignore it, or pretend it's not there. Clearly, there's some awful stuff that goes on. But what I am saying is that isn't the only story. So that's what I'm trying to do with it.

Why do you think it's important to share stories of kindness?

I found people were saying to me, 'I really like seeing the stuff you're doing about kindness' and I asked them, 'What is it you like?' And so many times people say it makes them feel more positive and gives them hope.

And what effect has doing this had on you?

I really enjoy doing it. I know I probably would notice a lot of these stories anyway, but I'm noticing more. And I love leading on something that is making a positive difference. One person said to me that seeing the stories literally saved his life, because when he was in a dark place, he couldn't see the kindness for himself. And I thought, yeah, this is too important not to do. I've got to do this. I've got to grow it. You know, I've had other people say to me, I see the world in a different way now, and you just think wow! Just from a little project that I've started.

Do you think that these kinds of stories belong in the news? And why do you think they aren't in the news?

Yeah, I think they should be there. You hear people saying, nobody's interested, you know. Bad news sells, those kinds of things. And I think to myself, how do you know if you don't publish positive stories? That just doesn't make sense. An area which I think illustrates it is the negative stories we get about leaders. But there are lots of leaders who lead with kindness as part of their practice. I think we don't hear about them so often, and this is where the news could play a role to showcase more of those positive role models and show young people examples of leading with kindness. Then they can think, I'm going to try it like that way, because I know I'll be successful.

What's one of your favourite stories of kindness?

There was a story my friend told me, where the automatic doors were broken in a shopping centre. There was an older lady with a walking frame trying to walk through. And there were people kind of streaming in towards her so she couldn't pass, and she had to have a little sit down. Then my friend stopped and helped her get through. And I really like that one, because it's easy to focus on the people who didn't help. But we can focus on the one person who was kind. We can choose to remember that bit. So it's not a massive story, but it's quite a nice illustration of that point.

It makes me think of that Lily Tomlin quote: 'I always wondered why someone doesn't do something about that. Then I realised I was somebody!'

Yes, we can all do something! I'm asking people to become Kindness Ambassadors by signing up on my website, and to make a pledge to notice at least one example of kindness once a week, and to tell at least one other person about it. I think we've got to keep that conversation going. We've got to get used to using the language of kindness and be comfortable with it. And it really did come from the idea of people wanting to know that they're not alone in believing in kindness and it's not weak and fluffy, despite what certain people will have you believe, that it's actually very strong and powerful.

Conversations on Kindness

In that thoughtful January I switched my 'New Year Resolutions' to 'New Year Revolutions'. Instead of 'giving things up', I decided to 'take things up'. For me this was the sharing of positive news stories, as well as stories of when I noticed or witnessed acts of kindness or received them myself. Instead of 'doing less of something', I decided to 'do more of something' by highlighting on my social media projects and people doing heart-warming, life-affirming things. Every January since, I have considered what positive things I can begin to do, and what positive things I am already doing of which I could do more. It's a much more celebratory way to begin the year. Kinder to myself and to everyone else.

7. FEBRUARY

What's Love Got to Do with It?

Five acts of kindness this month:

Day 169: I posted a box of treats to my friend's wife after they got burgled for the second time and she lost her wedding ring.

Day 175: I gave a jar of sweets to a nice man called Jamie who has been supporting Occupy outside St Paul's since the very beginning.

Day 179: I had a rendezvous with a man outside Deptford train station, who had asked me via Twitter to read him 'something I loved'. I read him The Nightingale and the Rose by Oscar Wilde. He was nice, I was nervous, it was a bit awkward, then it was good.

Day 192: I went to read stories to kids for Book Swap Day at Tea Dance for Little People in Brockley, a drop-in art club. I read this story I had written about some kids who discover a time machine in their mum's washing machine. Eventually we all agreed that blowing bubbles was a good idea, so that's what we did. We filled the room with bubbles, and all got a bit hysterical.

Day 195: I made and posted a card for Stewart Whoo, as suggested by my friend Denise Flower. A couple of weeks later, Stewart sent me this message on Facebook: 'As a recipient of one of your artworks, just want to thank you . . . and say it was successful. Quite emotional, shocking, bizarre and beautiful to get something so lovely out of the blue and with no reason. Truly magical.'

It was now about halfway through the year. I couldn't quite believe I had come this far. This month I made boxes filled with miniature scrolls of poetry and foil-wrapped chocolate coins and left them on park benches. I left geraniums in plant pots on people's doorsteps with labels saying, 'For you.' I left countless positive and anonymous reviews for books I had read, and cafes and pubs I had been to. Gareth was impressed.

He was also slightly alarmed at the amount of money I was spending, gently suggesting I should keep an eye on my outgoings. (Remember I was giving money to anyone who asked for it.) I added it up. It wasn't a *fortune*, but it was a lot to me. It wasn't very sustainable and, if I hoped to encourage people to continue joining in, not very persuasive either. I did start to think about other, more affordable, cheaper or even free ways of being kind apart from the 'writing online reviews and carrying shopping bags' kind.

Meanwhile, a date was looming that had already inspired me to plan my first large-scale act of kindness: Valentine's Day.

I've always thought it's great that we have a ready-made festival of love. When I first arrived in London, back in 1997, I made thirteen velvet Valentine's Day cards for friends I had been missing, and I kept with the tradition of Valentine anonymity, thinking it would be a magical and welcome thing to receive a beautiful handmade card. But I'm afraid it backfired in some cases as unfounded hopes were raised which were then dashed when I revealed myself as the sender.

That made me think about the failings and potentials of Valentine's Day. It's hazardous. And, let's be honest, it is a bit naff. The naffness itself is part of its charm — it's cute when you see burly men trailing heart-shaped helium balloons on the tube. But it is still largely heteronormative, mostly aimed at celebrating the love of monogamous straight couples, which seems a bit of a narrow remit to me. I wanted it to be a celebration of all kinds of love. For example, there's our love of our animal companions, or brinjal bhajis, or outdoor swimming, or the National Trust, or football. All those loves need to be celebrated too. And what about celebrating how much we love our friends and our work and how much we love laughing and dancing? This felt like an opportunity for kindness that I couldn't miss.

What's Love Got to Do with It?

So I approached this Valentine's Day with the intention of extravagantly celebrating it, and I wanted to make sure no one was left out (unless they wanted to be). To a serial adventurer like me, this felt utterly irresistible.

Come on, I thought, *let's reclaim V Day.*

So, I did just that. I shared my intention on social media to travel all over London on V Day giving away cards, cakes and gifts to total strangers, to celebrate love. I asked anyone who fancied it to join in however they liked. I assembled my small team of allies (in this case Asif Iqbal and Christine Entwisle, to whom I am eternally grateful). Chris agreed to film us on my little video camera. This was the first time I had made a focused effort to document anything I was doing, but I had a feeling the day was going to be epic.

Chris was also in charge of the route we were taking around London. She was interested in seeing how people reacted and 'the complexity of it'. Asif was a much newer friend, and he said he'd joined in because 'kindness was always something that really spoke to me, and it is always what I look for in people, too. I have often thought how there is not enough kindness in the world and maybe it is not spoken of enough, and when I read about what you were doing, and asked for people to join in, I just thought why not?'

So along he came, and we both made cards — his were adorned with beautiful quotes from the Persian poet Hafez, mine with pictures of Victorian cherubs I had cut out of an old scrapbook. I also made fifty rice crispy cakes with Swizzles love-heart sweets on top and blew up fifty heart-shaped balloons.

I wrote to the letters page of *Time Out* to tell them of our intentions, and they published it with the title 'Love Train'. They said they'd send a journalist along with us to see how it went, so we met Alexi Duggins at the *Time Out* offices in central London. Then off we went, to 'love bomb' London.

Conversations on Kindness

We travelled the whole day by tube and on foot; we gave away our cards and cakes on platforms, pavements, trains and stations; we visited the receptionists at Holloway Prison, gave a card and a cake to a person dressed in a promotional foam mobile phone costume in Camden, visited patrons of the bar of the Soho Theatre, laughed and drank with the punters of a French bistro called Beaujolais in the West End, and finished up in Hampstead where we met builders, tourists and an elderly milkman who said despite forty years of marriage he had never before received a Valentine's card. It was exhilarating, heart-warming, exciting, funny and exhausting.

We ended our day on Parliament Hill. After marching around Hampstead Heath giving away the last of our cards, cakes and balloons, we reached the bench on the top where you can look out across an epic view of London. I handed the very last balloon to a couple sitting on the bench. The woman told me it was unbelievable, because she had just a moment before asked her boyfriend to marry her! What a moment! What a day! Covered in mud, a little bit tipsy from the wine (I wasn't accustomed to daytime drinking), full of adrenaline and love for all people everywhere, I went home, satisfied that was mission completed.

I was absolutely buzzing. This was the first time I had experienced euphoria doing acts of kindness. I felt that I had seen for the first time what life could be like if you dare to live as if you are in a movie. (Not a movie like *Terminator*, obviously – more like a light-hearted romcom.) Of course even on this day there were moments when I was disappointed by rejections and irritated by rudeness, but the overwhelming majority of people were just overjoyed, delighted and so happy to talk about love and kindness. I could see people nearby watching and trying to take pictures or hear what we were doing. The batteries on my old camera ran out halfway through, so we couldn't document the rest, but it didn't matter. What did matter was that it had all been so joyful and uplifting.

What's Love Got to Do with It?

We had done it! We had reclaimed Valentine's Day! February 14 would never be the same again!

I count that day as the moment when the project really took off. It may have been the scale of it, the fact that I had by now been doing it for six months, but things changed after this. Shortly afterwards, Woolfson and Tay art gallery in Bermondsey approached me and asked if I would consider doing 'an exhibition of the work' at the end of the year. Magazines and newspapers asked me for interviews and features. It had never occurred to me that my daily acts of kindness would bring me that sort of fame or attention.

This had two major side effects, the first being that I got a lot more requests via social media from people asking me to do acts of kindness for friends or relatives of theirs who needed a bit of cheering up. I responded happily to all of these, mostly sending homemade cards, letters and gifts through the post. The second was that I got to meet Billy Bragg. I was invited on to the *Saturday Live* programme on BBC Radio 4, with Reverend Richard Coles, Sian Williams and Mr Bragg himself, to talk about what I had been up to and why. Billy was on to talk about his new album and to perform his hit 'Milkman of Human Kindness'. I made the three of them a Valentine's card each and took my ukulele in the hope that Billy might play the Milkman song on it for me, so I could learn the chords and play it myself sometime. (He kindly agreed — there's a video on YouTube of that spectacular moment!)

Lots of listeners rang and emailed in with their own very moving stories of acts of kindness, including a woman called Julie who told the incredible tale of when she crashed her car into a garden wall after her brakes failed. The occupants of the house responded by giving her tea, cake and the money to buy herself a new car, after she'd explained that 'this would be the end of her dream to be a midwife' because she needed the car to finish her training. She said the kindness of these strangers had a profound and long-lasting effect, as she was able to qualify and to 'spend the next thirty years in the best job in the world . . . I realise now how significant that little act of kindness was.'

From this I was reminded of how many people were doing far more to be kind than I was. But telling the stories of what I was doing, what I witnessed and experienced – that is what I could offer. Running around the streets of London giving out cakes and cards. Meeting strangers in the street and having proper conversations and recording them on socials and on my website. Writing up the ideas that really worked, that people could try for free, things that suited the shy or the bold, the skinted or the minted. I felt deeply and profoundly moved, as if I had found what I had been looking for at long last.

After that day, I thought a lot about the power and authority that fame lends you, how it gives you a platform and amplifies your voice, and how it is possible to use that for good. That's why many of us love people like Billy Bragg, not just for his music but also for his passions, his causes and what he believes in, for playing on picket lines and at protests and rallies. So, even if you only get fifteen minutes of fame, even if you are only famous in your own neighbourhood, you can use it for good, as he does.

Recently I contacted Billy, and he kindly agreed to chat with me about fame, kindness, empathy and his take on it all.

The Milkman of Human Kindness
with Billy Bragg

Your beautiful song 'The Milkman of Human Kindness' was a big inspiration for me. What was your intention with that song and what inspired you to write it?

Well, it's fundamentally a love song, so the inspiration for that comes from a lot of places. But I think that in a broader sense the currency of music is empathy. When you write a song, you are trying to get someone

What's Love Got to Do with It?

to feel some empathy for the subject matter that you're writing about, for the individual in the song perhaps. Or sometimes it's possible as a listener to draw some empathy from the song, because it makes you feel like the person who wrote the song has been reading your diary, and you can get some empathy from that. That's where kindness becomes political, it's empathy really that is the radical thing. Empathy is what underpins socialism. It is about imagining how you would feel if you had nothing, if you were in poverty, if you were a refugee, if you were a single mum. Empathy is not in and of itself political, but it is the underpinning of so much political activism.

There's a vulnerability in 'The Milkman of Human Kindness', too, which is what makes it so powerful.

Yes, and that vulnerability contrasts with the harder political stuff, that yin and yang of vulnerability and political toughness which has always been part of what I do. I think a lot of the attraction was that my politics were strong, but I wasn't trying to give the impression that I didn't have any doubts, that I was utterly sure of myself and that I was right, as I'm not that sort of person, so I don't know why I would pretend that. But I think a lot of people responded to that idea that you could be vulnerable, but you could also have ideals and cling to them as much as you could.

It really communicates throughout your work, the courage of laying out your frailties for everyone to see.

Yeah, well, they are the songs that most connect with people. Probably the most emotionally powerful song I ever wrote was 'Tank Park Salute', which was about the death of my father. People talk to me about that song all the time, it really gets people, and I'm glad because it really got me writing it, and it allowed me to say things that I hadn't really been able to say out loud since he died. So I think that if you can bear to be, as painful though it might be, as honest and vulnerable as you can, it connects with people more, rather than just singing platitudes.

I wanted to talk about one of your newer songs, 'I Will Be Your Shield', which really resonated with me...

I'll tell you why it resonated with you. It's basically a rewrite of 'Milkman of Human Kindness'... they're the same song, they're just coming at it from a different perspective.

I thought it was an interesting choice of words, because of our recent experience with Covid and shielding, and it works as it reminds us of the importance of looking after a person whom you love but also in a broader way of the importance of being kind and caring for each other.

Yes, and it's about solidarity as well, it's about standing together, whether you're talking in terms of personal, or in a much more societal level... we should work together to defend one another from 'the slings and arrows of outrageous fortune', as Shakespeare had it.

It feels like you've always used your talents to make the world a better place and to communicate messages. How important is message in your music?

It all depends on the context. What's the context of a song like 'There Is Power in a Union'? Well, yesterday I sang it for the teachers outside a school in Dorchester, a week before that I was singing it for ambulance drivers, a week before that I was out with the nurses – these things are crucial to what I do because they make the songs that I sing real. Next week when I'm in Australia singing that song I'll be trying to bring that picket-line vibe into the hall. I'm not a pop star coming to sing some of my songs, it's the context of those songs of solidarity and what they bring to the picket line, not just as entertainment, but also as a reminder that standing on a picket line is an old traditional way of ordinary working people getting organised.

What's Love Got to Do with It?

This particularly applies to where I live in Dorset, because we are close to the Tolpuddle Martyrs, who in 1834 were sentenced to transportation to Australia for forming a union, so music is the thing that threads it all together. 'There Is Power in a Union' is a song I wrote during the miners' strike [in 1984–5], and I sang it to a load of nurses who had never been on strike before, who weren't even born when the miners' strike happened, and so I'm able to say to them, 'Now you have stood on this picket line, you are part of that tradition, it doesn't matter what the context is, you are connected to the miners, and you are connected to the Tolpuddle Martyrs, and you are connected to the Suffragettes – and if this is your first time: welcome to the tradition.'

There's a first time for all of us, and so that aspect of it, you know, acting in solidarity with other people, that could be a sort of service which connects to empathy. You must have empathy in order to have solidarity, when you mix the empathy you have with the activism of going out and standing on a street in a picket line, that's when you get that really important aspect of solidarity, and that makes a difference.

Feeling plus action equals change.

Yes! Do you think we can put compassion, kindness and empathy at the heart of politics and policymaking?

I wrote a song about that a few years ago called 'Upfield', where I talk about 'socialism of the heart', which is different to 'socialism of the head'. Socialism of the heart is compassion, basically, where socialism of the head is ideology, and the two don't always match up – more often than not you get one without the other. If you don't get enough compassion in your ideology everything gets a bit dogmatic, so I've been hoping for a long time for greater compassion and more empathy.

As it has come up a lot in this conversation, could you tell me what your definition of socialism is?

Organised compassion. That's what it is. It's bringing together the people who are trying to make political change based on compassionate ideals. It has other elements as well which are just as important, like accountability – that must be a key aspect of it – and transparency, but fundamentally at its deepest the thing that shapes it, the thing that should guide the principle is organised compassion.

I am often told that kindness 'isn't enough', but for me it's the thing I come back to if I feel unsure of myself, as my north star. That may not be the answer for everybody, but I think it's important to have a 'north star' and I wondered if you have a guiding principle or set of principles like that?

Well . . . I'd say the last few years it has been the idea of accountability . . . am I accountable for what I am doing here? Regarding kindness . . . it's complicated . . . because it is not always a positive thing, is it? Sometimes it is the kinder thing to have your dog put down . . . it is a bit of a heartbreak, but that is the kind thing to do . . . so, kindness isn't always the easiest option . . . But the other thing is that the people who I have seen to have had a real problem with kindness are people who can't be kind to themselves . . . who can't see that we are all frail and that we are not here to judge them and you try to be kind to them, and it just upsets them . . . so although when you say kindness you think of puppies and kittens, but it's quite a volatile thing, isn't it? Depending on whether you can handle it or not.

I'm considering what radical kindness means and looks like, and I was thinking that if we dare to put kindness, compassion and empathy at the centre of policymaking decisions and acknowledge radical kindness – kindness that 'demands institutional change' – do you think that it can effectively be part of making the world a better place moving forward?

Well, if we are talking about building bridges with our political opponents, unfortunately there's been a tendency on the right in the past few

What's Love Got to Do with It?

years to see any kind of empathy, compassion or kindness as a weakness, and something to be derided. You know, you've only got to talk about your concern for any minority group and that can be dismissed. They've got a whole armoury of tropes to dismiss you, everything from 'politically correct' which comes from the 1980s to the more recent 'woke'. These are all terms that are deployed to attack kindness, to portray any sense of fellow feeling as a fundamental threat to our way of life. It's very hard to talk to people like that from a position of kindness, from a position of empathy, because they don't see kindness, they see weakness; they don't see compassion, they see a threat, they have a very narrow definition of the way society should work. And the idea of putting down their guard, and allowing the possibility not even that other people are right but that other people have a right to actually speak, is sometimes too much for them.

That's always been there, it is just that in the 1970s and 80s that was done in the pages of our daily newspapers, that dismissal of empathy, and it still goes on. You must ensure that there's a safe space to be able to discuss things without being attacked, whether you are coming from the left or coming from the right. In that space, then you can have that kind of discussion, but we're not in that place at the moment.

Maybe we can't have those conversations on Twitter or other platforms which require immediate responses, and brief responses?

Yes, it doesn't have to be a literal space, of course, it could be a psychological space. I wrote a book a couple of years ago called *The Three Dimensions of Freedom* in which I argued that in order to have a discourse that is reasonable you need three things to be present: liberty – the right to express your view; equality – your willingness to listen to other people's point of view; and accountability – the willingness of both sets of participants not to behave in a way that is abusive or derogatory. Being offensive is probably allowed, but a safe space doesn't stop you from saying what you want to say, it just referees the way you want to say it. It ensures that everybody gets to speak, that nobody gets shouted down, that nobody gets bullied. That's the point of a safe space: it's not to control the debate. If you can't put your opinion across without being abusive, without being a bully, then you really don't deserve the opportunity to speak in that space. Go and find another space to speak — there's plenty of them. But in this space, we respect these rules, and everybody has equal weight to what they are saying, and we speak together, and we are accountable for what we do, so it's trying to create that atmosphere in which something like kindness then can come to the fore, and not be seen as a threat.

What would you say to someone who is despairing of the state the world is in, someone who wants to do something and doesn't feel like anything they could do would make any sort of difference?

Learn to play a guitar, write songs, do gigs — find a way to get it out of your system. It's very therapeutic, playing a musical instrument. Songs allow you to say things you can't put into words. For example, 'The Milkman of Human Kindness' would sound stupid as a conversation, but as a song it works. Music gives you licence to use a metaphor as silly as a milkman walking around delivering kindness. I mean, it's a stupid idea, isn't it? But in the context of the song it has power, the message is more powerful than the stupid image. And I like the stupidness of it — you can hit people with a smile with that song.

Shortly after this, Billy went off to get his hair cut ready for his tour, and I considered how we could cultivate kindness as a political virtue, by centring it in our own lives and by expecting it as a core value of our political leaders. If kindness was central to political policymaking, if the happiness of all humans and more-than-human beings was paramount,

What's Love Got to Do with It?

then a more peaceful, free and just society would be inevitable, surely? I thought about how our behaviour to those nearest and dearest to us matters too, that with our values and our actions, as well as who we vote for and who we support, we should always strive to be kind, and that this effort could bring us to an authentically kind world. And that as strange as it feels to think and to write, in the political landscape we currently find ourselves in, politics can be and should be kind.

8. MARCH

People Ain't No Good

Five acts of kindness this month:

Day 197: I donated to New Cross People's Library for World Book Day. The library had been shut down due to cuts and reopened by the community.

Day 202: I delivered some treats and a thank-you card to the Waiting Room cafe staff in Deptford.

Day 204: International Women's Day! I bought a lottery ticket, put it in a gold envelope and handed to a smiley woman in the library.

Day 219: I saw a woman struggling with a case and helped her carry it up the stairs at the station.

Day 226: During our show I gave a woman in the audience a bunch of hyacinths. She tweeted me later to let me know she had shared them with another lady on the bus who liked them.

I had never really dealt with my experiences as a child — the rejection by my dad, and the abuse from my stepdad — or faced the pain and damage they had caused me. I'd never been offered or received counselling, never joined any therapy groups or read any self-help books. I'd soldiered on, regardless, telling myself I was fine, I was indomitable, there was nothing I couldn't deal with. But I began to realise that every time I experienced rejection (and I had chosen a profession that pretty much guaranteed I faced it regularly), I felt the pain of my dad's rejection again, like a blade in my heart.

I wasn't great at bouncing back. I took rejection very personally and spent days in bed eating packets of biscuits and hiding from everyone. The unworthiness and shame I felt because of the childhood abuse I had experienced sometimes floored me too, in the same way.

All human beings experience self-doubt. That self-doubt can be helpful, it can motivate you to learn and keep growing. But my self-doubt was brutal, in that I wondered if there was any point in me being alive at all, as I was so utterly worthless.

Thankfully, it didn't usually last, and once the storm had passed I locked it away somewhere deep inside and did my very best to ignore it. But it reared its head now, in the aftermath of the adventures of Valentine's Day, once the adrenaline left me. I told myself that what I was doing was pointless, it wasn't really making any difference to anyone, it might even be irritating people, that I should just let it go. There are people who give away their kidneys, take bullets for strangers, run into burning buildings to rescue dogs. Huge awe-inspiring self-sacrificing things that I hadn't done. All I did was give people strange and eccentric gifts, leave bunches of flowers in cafes, write poems on pavements in parks – nice, but what good was it really doing? It still hadn't diminished any of those huge troubles in the world that had motivated me to start this.

As lovely as the encouragement via social media was – and it *was* encouraging to notice good things – it was still true that terrible, awful things were happening in the world. If I really thought that kindness could change the world, then *how*? Could it really help make peace and stop war?

I guess this was bound to happen sooner or later. That despite the euphoria and the adventures, the positive feedback and the fun that I was having, this inner critic would come to whisper in my ear. I had underestimated both how rewarding and how exhausting this whole project would be. Money was tight, time was tighter and I was always on a train, lugging an obscenely huge suitcase up and down stairs.

People Ain't No Good

Something different happened this time, though. It was almost as if I spoke back to the voice of self-doubt in my head. It seemed that focusing on kindness had strengthened me, had given me something tangible to counter the doubt with. I resolved to continue, if not for any other reason than that I had said I would.

My eyes had been opened to kindness and to suffering, to pain and to joy. One day I met a man called Terry in Soho. I had been visiting my friend Celine, and I had a bunch of wildflowers which I had tried to give to a woman passing by. She smiled, but said she didn't want them. This didn't happen often — mostly flowers got a great reception — but sometimes it did, and it was always a bit gutting. I reminded myself that not everyone would say yes, and that's okay, that — as the saying goes — 'everyone is fighting a battle you know nothing about', and just as I was thinking this, I saw a man sitting on the floor with a cardboard sign which said: 'HUNGRY AND HOMELESS. PLEASE HELP.'

I offered the man the flowers, plus new some socks and a cereal bar. By this point I had taken to carrying around things that might be helpful to people living on the street. He said thanks, and told me that no one in his whole life had given him flowers before. He showed me a Cornish pasty that he said he had found on the top of a bin, with just one tiny bite out of it, and asked me if I thought it was all right if he ate it. I said yes. And then, as I said goodbye and turned to walk away, I considered what I had just said to him.

'No! No, I'm so sorry, don't eat that. I'll buy you another,' I said, and went to buy him a pasty.

He thanked me profusely. I thanked him for being so friendly and for accepting the flowers. We introduced ourselves. I blinked when he said Terry. That was my stepdad's name. I felt a dark fizz in my guts, but I remember thinking, *Well, it's good to meet a nice person called Terry at least.*

This is how our conversation went:

Conversations on Kindness

Terry: You are kind.

Me: Oh, no, it's fine, you're welcome. I'm sorry it's not more.

Terry: You wouldn't help me if you knew who I am. I mean, what I have done.

Me: Oh no, I don't think that's true.

Terry: I don't deserve it. I have got what I deserve, and I accept it. I went to prison, you see. Which is the worst thing that can happen to anyone. But I should have gone to prison, and I did go. I'll probably die out here. But I'm no use to anyone, so that is okay.

This was a long way away from the sweet and amusing exchanges I was used to having on the street. And it was so upsetting, this broken man in front of me with the same name as my abuser, telling me that he deserved to go to prison. I asked myself what use were a pair of socks and a cereal bar to someone in so much obvious pain? And I couldn't help but wonder what he had done, although I didn't want to know. I was frightened to know, in case I discovered that if I knew, I would behave differently towards him. We chatted a little more. I wasn't sure what to say, so I offered him a few words of comfort, told him to take care of himself, gave him some money and wandered off.

I walked through the streets of Soho for a while afterwards, trying to process what had just happened and what had come up as a result.

Terry told me he had 'done bad things' and 'hurt people'. Other homeless people I met had told me things like they had 'brought things on myself by drinking' – each seemed to have internalised a pernicious view of their situation, that some people do not deserve help because their choices and actions have led them to where they are. This is an unkind and unhelpful oversimplification of what can happen in any life, to anyone. The woman who chooses a man who then beats her, who then runs away, becoming homeless as a result, has made, you could say, 'terrible' choices. The man who self-medicates with alcohol to ease his

People Ain't No Good

pain and shame and ends up jobless and on the streets has equally made 'terrible' choices, but neither of them sought to be in that position. We can all make poor or misguided choices, but some of us have safety nets that others don't: money, or family, or friends who can help. Some people have the prejudices of society stacked against them, making it harder to get back to work, get a home, access guidance and support. In a hostel I stayed in for a short while in the 1990s I met people like me who had made bad decisions, but we were able to start again due to the beneficence of a welfare system which at that time still provided the chance of secure and affordable housing. So I can't and didn't judge anyone I met. But that man in Soho, maybe because his name was Terry, and the association that had for me, maybe because he muttered darkly that he had hurt people: he challenged me, and I found myself having dark, gloomy thoughts. For the first time I wondered if there are people who do such terrible things that they are undeserving of kindness.

Before I left, Terry had said to me, 'Hurt people hurt people. Have you heard that saying?' I hadn't, but it stayed with me. I went seeking words of wisdom around this topic: how we can and should be kind to people who may have hurt people, and I came across this from author Will Bowen: 'People hurt others as a result of their own inner strife and pain. Avoid the reactive response of believing they are bad; they already think so and are acting that way. They aren't bad; they are damaged, and they deserve compassion.'

That meeting with Terry didn't make me go to bed to hide and eat biscuits, but it did make me feel sad and worried. I thought about prison, and what it had done to Terry. In my heart I knew that everyone deserves kindness. No matter what they have done or the circumstances in which they find themselves. In that case, was there a better way for society to deal with those who break the law? Might there even be a way for prison to be kind, so that the people there might heal? Or I was just being hopelessly naïve?

Conversations on Kindness

Years ago, I was lucky enough to work with Sandra Barefoot. Sandra is an artist, a creative thinker, an academic and, as she describes herself, a 'researcher of life'. At the time we met she lived near me in South East London, and we were both performers in Cardboard Citizens, the theatre company for people who had experienced homelessness. She moved to Bristol when her sons were small, and we lost touch. But I'd kept up with her work and I knew she was working on a prison project called Restore with the Forgiveness Project. I wanted to get her expert opinion on how we can be kind to everyone, including those who have made mistakes, fallen through the cracks and ended up on the streets, or in prison, or vulnerable in other ways. Alongside her, I wanted to explore what could be changed about the system that resulted in the broken man I met in Soho.

Let Me Tell You How I Was
with Sandra Barefoot

Sandra, could you tell me a little about your work with Restore and its aims?

Restore is an intensive group-based prison programme, led by a team of highly skilled facilitators and speakers who share their lived experiences of being harmed and/or of inflicting harm upon others and having served in prison as a result. We support people in the process of change towards desistance from crime.

And I believe you use stories or a narrative approach to help with this?

Yes, we use the narrative approach to look at the possibilities of living a life differently to how we've lived it before. The aims are really to shift perspectives, by telling and sharing stories that heal, restore and rehumanise. It's exploring how we connect and understand each other, so we know that we're not alone. We are stepping into the shoes of others, so it's about compassion and empathy. It's a deep and complex programme.

People Ain't No Good

It's about stories, our experiences and what is it to be human – and how did we get here?

Do you find it effective?

It never fails. It's so simple. You're in a circle, and you're sharing parts of who you are, with no guard up. So you're vulnerable, and you're finding courage. It's the oldest place to be in the world, isn't it? Just in a circle with people, sharing stories. The prisoners used to say, 'How is this possible that we able to share our stories here?' Because there's nowhere else that is safe enough for them to do that.

Why do you think that telling their stories is important for the participants?

One of the reasons is if you've never been recognised, witnessed or acknowledged in your whole life for what you've been through, you need to be. That's the medicine for each one of us. I think that's the fundamental thing. Secondly, I think people have nowhere to be listened to and to be heard, especially in prison. The crime you did, it's written on flat paper. You are seen as a horrendous person. You have no right to rectify that. So there's something really important about being able to present and share your whole self. You need to be able to say, 'Let me tell you about how I was as a boy. This is why the boy became this . . .' It allows something to open in your heart and your thoughts about yourself, how people see you, and how you're seeing yourself.

It's just so emotional. You can be seen and heard without any judgement. People will say, 'I have never ever spoken about that in my life. I can't believe I could even share that to a group of strangers. And that you have all held me with so much care and love.' Because that's what it brings, I mean it's profound. You have men walking across to hug each other. It's re-humanising yourself while you're doing it, and you get these connections with those that you would never have dreamed you might connect with.

There was this guy, he was from Syria, and he'd walked across so many continents to flee war. No one knew his story. He cried in the group as he shared how lonely he was in his cell and he didn't have any connection to the other people on the wing. When he stood up to tell his story, the men were astonished by his journey and just wrapped themselves around him, with compassion and care. At the end of the programme this man said, 'I'm not alone anymore. I'm not crying on my own.' That is profound, isn't it?

Yes, it really is immensely powerful and moving. Do you find that there are things that recur often when people tell stories?

There's so much loss, there's so much grief. There's so much death. You could say the whole prison system is a grave, I mean it's just shocking. It's just not spoken about. It leaves me speechless. So you'll always have the death of the divorce, the death of the father leaving home, death of friends and a lot of violence in the home, especially male violence towards women. For women serving in prison, the statistics are so high for women who have suffered domestic violence and or sexual abuse. I find it so insulting when women share their stories that there has been no justice served in the harm done to them. It's just not okay that women are in prison when they have never received justice for the horrific abuse they have experienced. It's wrong. And they get double the rate of sentencing. They get much harsher and longer sentencing than men.[1]

There's a lot connected to shame here, too. Women are judged by many people more harshly. It might be when I, as a woman, look to

---

[1] Statistics bear her out here. According to womeninprison.org.uk, 'More women are being sent to prison when 69 per cent of them have committed a non-violent crime . . . The women's prison population is predicted to rise 16 per cent by November 2027 . . . the root causes of what drives women's contact with the criminal justice system include poverty, a chronic lack of safe, suitable housing, and poor mental health.'

People Ain't No Good

another woman, and she represents something that I feel shame about, I'm going to be harsh on her. It's almost like a mirror is being put up that we do not want to see and so we defend ourselves and say, 'I'm not that kind of woman. I will separate myself from that. I never want to be associated with you, and I'll shame you so badly for who you are.' So, I think to be radically kind is to understand what's going on with our own shame and how this leads us to respond to people in certain ways. We need to nurture compassion, empathy and understanding instead for ourselves and others.

I keep thinking that prisoners are one of the communities that most need compassion and kindness, and yet they receive it less.

Yes, that's the unkindest thing. Radical kindness is to know that you're going into an arena that is so nuanced, so complex, that you cannot tar everybody with one brush. You need to see and rehumanise each person as an individual who has unique life experience. Be curious to consider what happened to them, what led them to this place and what will help them to be a 'returning citizen' and restore their faith in their humanity and in ours.

There are many acts of kindness in prison that are often not known about. There are prison officers who do many things for people, like buying clothes out of the catalogues or sorting out Christmas gifts. And it's the small everyday interactions on the wings, simply asking, 'Are you ok?', that makes the difference. I remember one woman telling me that when she received terrible news that a prison officer said to her, 'I'll give you a hug. I'm not meant to give you a hug. But I'm going to hug you right now. I'm just going to tell you I see you and you're really brave.' All these lovely little things happen all the time.

It's so good to hear that, yet again it reinforces my belief that very small acts can be incredibly powerful.

There was something recently I wanted to tell you, something here that relates to the Black Lives Matter movement. A speaker at our symposium said that things are changing now because middle class white people are getting arrested and getting into trouble. So, they're starting to realise what prison is like, what the criminal justice system is like, and its failings and shortcomings. So, this speaker was saying, perhaps we don't have to shout anymore now, as other people are doing the shouting... because finally, other kinds of people are having these experiences.

Most people just don't know the reality of prison or of leaving prison. You know people leaving prison are just dropped at a bus stop. They walk out the prison with their plastic bag, and their £46, some of them are back in prison in no time. They have no support network and nowhere to go. In America they are called 'returning citizens'. We call them ex-offenders. And calling people that keeps them in that identity. It's an unwanted identity that you just can't get rid of.

I wonder if you could share with us a story of someone who for you was really transformed by the process of Restore?

There are so many! But let me tell you the story of one young guy who was so desperate to change, but when he came to the programme, he was very resistant to it to begin with. But when we tried a visual art exercise, I saw the joy in him coming out. He said, 'I've not done anything like this since I was a child,' and at the end of the programme, he said, 'This has changed the way I see myself and others.' I wrote a detailed report about what I'd witnessed and seen in him. As he read it in front of the whole group, he was emotional and said, 'I have never ever received any validation before in my whole life.' He asked for another copy to send to his girlfriend and said 'She's never seen me written about in this way. And when I get out, I'm going to frame it.' That really touched me because he was so young, twenty-six or twenty-seven years old. That was gold.

People Ain't No Good

I just keep coming back to the thought and the need to accept that it is really complicated to be human.

Absolutely. But people will say it's not that complicated. You just need to stick to the rules in your life.

But there's not one set of rules for everyone!

I think that's why it's so complex. Whose rules are you standing by? Who made the rules? Are the rules fair or the same for everyone? We have to ask these questions.

I thought back to the man called Terry I met on the street, and how much hurt and pain he expressed; I wondered what prison had been like for him, and what had landed him there. And because of the strange coincidence of his name, and of him telling me he 'hurt people', I inevitably thought about my stepdad again too. I realised that I did not know his story, who he 'was as a boy'. Or 'why the boy became this', as Sandra put it.

I didn't know what he'd suffered, or what had happened to him to make him so cruel and harmful. Everything inside me rebelled against this thought, for myself, my sisters, my mum and for all other survivors. I did not want to be compassionate to him right then. I was a long way away from being ready to process the idea that I might think kindly towards the person who had caused me and my family so much damage, and even further from any idea of forgiveness. But the seed was planted here.

If 'hurt people hurt people', then perhaps it was also true that 'healed people can heal people'. Perhaps this is what I could offer, in the future – the story of how I healed myself in the hope that it might help other people to heal themselves. It was something to think about, for sure.

9. APRIL

Born to Run

> *Five acts of kindness this month:*
>
> **Day 244:** I carried a spare umbrella in case anyone got caught in today's torrential rain. It was leopard print. I found someone in brolly need at my friend's burlesque class.
>
> **Day 247:** I sent a card and a gift through the post for my friend's nan's best friend who needed cheering up.
>
> **Day 250:** On World Book night I was invited to speak about 366 Days of Kindness at Manor House library. I decided to ask them to try an act of kindness by paying each other compliments. They did this with such enthusiasm that it was very difficult for me to get their attention back. Then I gave an audience member a plant.
>
> **Day 253:** I went to see the play *Kafka's Monkey*, starring Kathryn Hunter. I left her an anonymous card saying, 'Well done, you're great.'
>
> **Day 257:** I helped a lady with a massive case onto the train to Brighton. I shouted, 'Holy ****', as it was so heavy. Then I said, 'I'm very sorry for swearing.' But I doubt even the Isle of Wight weighs as much as that case.

April, and a huge event was on the horizon – the mighty London Marathon. Thousands of people raising funds for good causes would be running past my door, and my partner Gareth would be one of them.

I love a grand gesture, putting on a bit of a show/having a party, and this was the month to do it. I'd lived on the eight-mile mark of the London Marathon route since 1997, and had stood and cheered people on every year, but now it felt like it might be time to go large. Gareth was running it for the first time, raising funds for Children with Cancer for his niece who had been very ill with leukaemia as a child. He'd trained hard for a whole year, through rain and snow and minor injuries.

If you are lucky enough to live on a marathon route, you'll know it's like a New Year's Eve party beginning very early in the morning. In previous years my neighbours Tap and Brutal, two fantastic grizzly punk DJs, had built a huge sound system a few doors away to entertain the runners, and it was fantastic. There'd been Morris dancers outside the McDonald's down the road, and kids wandering up and down the road selling homemade biscuits to raise money for charities.

So a few weeks before the big day, I decided to post on social media to ask anyone with a friend, relative or colleague running to let me know I pledged to paint them personalised banners and put them on display in my window, so when they ran past at the eight-mile mark they would hopefully see them and be surprised and encouraged. I bought paper bunting and pompoms, made a marathon playlist, bought a huge number of sweets, chocolates and oranges, and filled the fridge with ice. I opened the toilet to the public with a sign saying 'TOILET HERE'. (This was a mistake. The toilet was trashed, not in a Glastonbury Festival way, but more in an 'Andrex puppy trails of toilet paper everywhere' way.) I brought out chairs to our tiny front yard and when I got up super early to climb a ladder and put up the posters and the bunting, I said hello and chatted to everyone who went by.

My sisters and I set up a free cocktail bar and made raspberry bellinis and vegan sausage sandwiches for anyone who wanted one. It was a festival vibe, cheery and so exciting. I sat drinking a mimosa as Gordon Ramsay came running by my house, not something that happens every day. A short while after the elite runners had passed, lean and fast as greyhounds, the huge mass of everyday runners came along. Together with friends and family who had come to lend their support, I shouted myself hoarse.

People tend to wear their names on their tops, so it was easy to call out, 'Go on, Caleb!' and 'You can do it, Helen' and so on. We filled endless small bowls with sweets and orange quarters which got snatched up and gulped down. Later came the dispensing of ice cubes and impromptu showers from a watering can prepared in advance. We managed to spot pretty much all the runners we had made banners for, and they all seemed delighted. Neighbours sat with us, strangers came and stood by our wall and joined in the loud encouragement. At one point I found myself calling out, 'These are the last flumps in South East London!' It was an amazing morning.

Gareth came by making excellent time, at which point I abandoned the house and went to meet him further on in the run. He finished at a very respectable five hours and twenty minutes and was very pleased.

It had been such a beautiful day. I'd spoken to neighbours who I hadn't met before and who have remained firm friends. I received messages of thanks from people for whom we had painted banners. I was reminded about the power of community connection, which is not without its challenges on a busy main road in London with a partly transitory community — but it's possible. I was reminded not to miss any chances for joy. It seemed easy to be kind to strangers, to friends and to neighbours that day because it was such fun.

This joyfulness reminded me of a very particular feeling I'd had one day after an act of kindness. I was on a train, and I'd ended up having a conversation with a man, just a very ordinary but nice, friendly conversation, and he told me he'd lost his wallet. I gave him some money, and when we finished our conversation and he got off the train I experienced this incredibly intense euphoria. Everything appeared brighter and more vivid, as if the world was suddenly in Technicolor. I felt both peaceful and exhilarated. It probably lasted for about twenty minutes. Or it could have been one minute. It was almost overwhelming, and I felt a bit teary, and afterwards I wondered, 'What on earth was that?'

There'd been other highs, too, such as on the day I gave everyone Valentine's cards, but this stuck out because of the strength of the experience triggered just by me talking to this man on a train.

This rekindled my curiosity about the neuroscience of kindness. I wanted to know what was going on inside my brain and body that meant that being kind felt so good. And given that it does feel so good, then why is it not literally prescribed on the NHS as a way of combating all sorts of ills, including sadness, loneliness and despair?

So, first stop was Dr David Hamilton. I bought his book *Why Kindness Is Good for You* to help me begin to understand what had been going on for me this year, and what the buzz of Marathon Day was about. From his work I first learned about oxytocin, one of the 'molecules of kindness', which has many positive benefits such as reducing blood pressure, helping to counter stress and reducing inflammation. Kindness, according to Dr Hamilton's research, relaxes the nervous system, guiding it into 'rest and relax', and diminishes the risk of heart disease by reducing free radicals in the arteries and immune system. So, kindness protects the cardiovascular system. Which means that doing something from the 'goodness of your heart' can literally protect your heart!

As well as oxytocin (also known as the 'love hormone', because it gives us a rush of pleasure from experiencing affection and connection), there are other 'happy hormones': dopamine, which gives us feelings of reward and motivation; serotonin, which is a mood-stabiliser and helps us regulate feelings of happiness and wellbeing; and endorphins, which alleviate pain, lower stress levels and support feelings of wellbeing too.

I loved beginning to understand what was going on in my brain when I carried out acts of kindness.

During this period, I also discovered several people and organisations who were promoting kindness, and reached out to them via social media. I had tea and chats about kindness with the director of Action for Happiness, Mark Williamson; David Jamilly, the founder of Kindness UK; and Sanderson Jones from Sunday Assembly. I loved being connected with and having conversations with people doing the same kind of thing. I began to feel like I had found a community and realised that this was what I had been missing.

Much later, I was lucky enough to meet experimental psychologist and cognitive neuroscientist Dr Dan Campbell-Meiklejohn when we were both invited to be guests on BBC *Sunday Morning Live* with Holly Hamilton and Sean Fletcher. Like Dr Gillian Sandstrom, Dr Campbell-Meiklejohn works with the University of Sussex Centre for Research on Kindness. He has had an amazing journey from his working-class roots in Canada to being interested in and studying philosophy and psychology, travelling in Europe, bartending in Ireland, couch-surfing in London and eventually getting a scholarship to Oxford University, where he did his PhD. He and I have taken very different routes with our study of kindness, and I was really excited to get his perspective on what was going on inside my brain when carrying out kind acts.

Helper's Highs
with Dr Dan Campbell-Meiklejohn

So, just to start us off, could I ask how do you define kindness?

I always thought kindness was a soft word and I'd like to make it as strong a word as hero. I'd like us to realise that it takes strength to be kind. I would define kindness as performing an action that can make someone else's life better or reduce their suffering. That's really it. It can be small or big. I don't think it requires some pure notion of altruism or anything like that. I don't think it has to be completely selfless. It's just doing things that make other people's lives better than they were before.

Conversations on Kindness

I've had one strikingly vivid and intense feeling of euphoria after carrying out an act of kindness – I can remember it in great detail and it had a huge impact on me. I wonder if you have any thoughts about what might have been going on?

I often think about acts of kindness as only having tiny effects on our wellbeing. They're little and gradually they add up. It's like doing exercise – you never get a result right away. It's a cumulative effect which gradually impacts your life positively, right?

But, I can also relate. I had an experience like that when I was like nineteen years old, and I remember it like it was yesterday. I was brought up Catholic, but I don't really go to church usually. But on this occasion, I was going to meet my friends in a pub around the corner for a drink later, so before that I popped into a church. There was this big man, a couple of pews over. He was so distraught, he was just crying and crying, so I went over to him and asked, 'How's it going? Do you need to someone to talk to?' This man was probably twenty years older than me, and he was clearly a builder – he had big, rough hands. He told me that he had just come from the hospital, where he had witnessed the passing of his mother. He was obviously suffering and he was burdened with knowledge of what had just happened. So we went and talked together over a pitcher of beer. I didn't try to give him any answers, I just listened. And after he left, I felt absolutely like you described. I think I had this wave of knowing I have this ability to have a positive impact on someone's life. It felt meaningful. I never saw him again. I hope he's okay. And that experience inspired me to volunteer as a counsellor in my early days.

I wonder what might have been going on in my brain, or your brain, in those moments, in terms of chemistry? As I understand it, our bodies reward us when we do kind things: we get a 'helper's high'. So was what we experienced simply an intense version of that?

There are a lot of things that make us feel good and exhilarated in the moment: oxytocin, for example, helps us feel bonded to other people. Endorphins give you the sensation of reward and dopamine helps you learn to do that rewarding thing again. The brain is a learning machine, really. So when you have something that makes you feel good, like eating something delicious, or doing something nice for someone, you remember the satisfaction and this allows you to predict that a good thing is about to happen if you do that good thing again. The reward you feel helps you make that association, as long as you know where that good feeling came from.

So, for example, I might be about to give someone a bunch of flowers, and the association I have from a previous experience of doing this is that the recipient is going to be surprised, delighted and grateful. So I get a buzz from the anticipation of the response?

Yes, we are built to teach ourselves to do the things that bring us satisfaction and help us stay alive. Being nice to others helps us all survive, it helps us form bonds that keep protective groups together. So it is no surprise we get rewarded for seeing others lives get better, especially lives we decide to care about. But I also think there's a lot in your experience, the pleasure we get from doing something kind for someone, that affirms to ourselves that we exist with meaning. This is getting philosophical, but I think we get intrinsic satisfaction from affecting things in our worlds, like a confirmation that we are here, and we matter.

I think the best method of finding meaning is positively influencing other people. So the feeling one gets from being kind can be comforting, empowering and reinforcing. I don't think neuroscience has caught up to all this yet. But talk to me in ten years! I hope we'll come closer to it. As for the rush you felt: I couldn't label it as specifically dopamine or serotonin or anything like that because we weren't scanning your brain at the time, but I would be very curious to find out what that feeling is myself.

I have experienced lots of pleasant feelings associated with daily acts of kindness, but that particular time was very intense. So it made a lasting impression.

Absolutely. Have you thought about whether there was anything about that particular interaction that had meaning for you or was there a moment where you thought, 'This is me now. This is what I do?'

Yes, you know I think there was that. And I think there was a growing, deep understanding of the real interconnectedness of the whole world. And somehow I felt that, in that moment.

So that sounds like something happened internally in you. If you can switch from what might be a more pessimistic view of things to the view that people are good, and if there's a feeling of interconnectedness, then it's possible, when you make that switch, that your expectations of the future change dramatically, and that can suddenly give you a great anticipation that there's a reward coming, together with a release of anxiety.

So there are two things happening there. I think both of those things together can be very synergistic, and be a visceral sense of excitement and relief. A change of perspective can be very powerful for changing your expectations of how life can be.

Do you feel that studies into kindness have proved that it is beneficial for us?

From what I understand from the meta-analysis of the effect on our wellbeing of being kind, I think the consensus is that kindness is rewarding to the kind person. But I think the benefits might be described as quite small. I think experiences like you had are probably quite rare, but when they do happen, they are very impactful. The most recent experience I had like that was when my first-born child was born, and I was in the room with my wife when she was in labour. It was immense and overwhelming. It felt very hormonal! It resulted in an incredible sense of compassion for my wife and my baby. It was about hope for the future, it was about meaning, it was caring. It was all the things mixed up. I found it close to the experience of being in love. And I think if we can find that feeling in everyday interactions – well then, we will be very happy people! But usually, as I say, studies have shown that acts of kindness create small changes that add up to a sense of well-being. We can't always expect to have this great visceral moment, we can think about it like exercise – one small improvement at a time.

I think it's also important to think about the neuroscience in terms of it's not only about the wellbeing you get from doing the kind thing, but also about the alternative, doing the selfish things, that can give you feelings of guilt. It's good to consider how you feel doing that kind thing, relative to how you feel doing the unkind, selfish thing. But there are so many reasons to be kind. A good feeling is just one, but the reason that good feeling is there is usually a better one. We evolved to have that feeling because it makes our life and the lives of others better. But maybe remembering the little buzz is also enough to tip the scales for some people.

Do you think some people could be persuaded into kind behaviour more easily if they knew the neuroscience behind it? If they understood about the rewards?

Well, there is a power to neuroscience that gives people something to anchor a decision on. People consider that biology is something intrinsic, something beyond their control. So it's an authority. People are drawn to ideas of behaviours that are natural, or the ideas that maybe civilisation is making us behave in certain ways, so let's go back to what we're supposed to be doing, which is a more natural way of doing things. The next part of the argument is we evolved to do this or that. But if we evolved to do this or that, there must be a purpose to it, there must be a benefit to us. So that's kind of the logic I tend to use, that the reward of kindness must be there for a reason. If we've lost touch with that reason, that's a problem. But maybe if we start doing more kindness, each of us will figure out what that reason is.

It feels powerful to invite people to try acts of kindness themselves, to see for themselves what effect it has on them.

Yes, and it doesn't matter whether it's purely altruistic or not. I think every act that we do needs to be motivated, and that motivation must come from a reward. There's no way you're going to get away from some seemingly selfish interpretation. And that's okay. But your actual reasons and rewards for doing kind things can still be because you value the benefits to other people, right? That still makes you a 'good' person in my book.

I think you can argue yourself out of an act of kindness by thinking it's not altruistic, it is not selfless enough. I don't think it matters, if you're doing something because you want to help somebody else, which will also make you feel good.

I think we can celebrate that we do it to make people feel good, and if that makes you feel good, then great. And if it didn't, you wouldn't do it. So, it's way better for it to make you feel good too. People wouldn't be helping others if it always made them unhappy.

No, it would not be sustainable. And the way I think to persuade people to try it, is to share the powerful stories of the impact of kindness and share the interesting and amazing things that are happening inside your brain.

Yes, they need to go together, 100 per cent. It's quite a lot of dry stuff without stories and feelings to make it interesting, but I think there's also people that are going to be persuaded more by one or the other. So the more we work together, the better, and the more people we are going to reach.

Born to Run

In the afterglow of Marathon Day, I decided make it a tradition. So I did. I've done the same pretty much every year since, sitting on the steps making mocktails and cocktails for friends and neighbours and giving away hundreds of sweets. My friend and neighbour Joyce helps me hand out treats and encouragement; my octogenarian friend Dorothy, who lives in the flats opposite, comes to dance wildly in the street; the Patel family who run our corner shop Krishna News supply all the goodies; my neighbour's grandson dances on top of our front wall; and Theresa next door calls out encouragement from her balcony like a gorgeous Irish Juliet. The streets are lined with people cheering on strangers and loved ones. We've made posters for lots of people now. So, if you're reading this and you're planning to run the marathon, get in touch, and we will do our best to make you a sign. If you're running past the eight-mile mark, you might even get a sweet.

10. MAY

Compliment Slips

Five acts of kindness this month:

Day 260: I helped two very nervous tourists who told me that they had never travelled via escalator before, making them laugh and giving them sweets to suck to help take their minds off the huge travelling staircase.

Day 267: I left a postcard with an encouraging message inside a book at WH Smith's.

Day 268: Today someone on a motorbike tried to steal my phone and my bag out of my hand, but I stubbornly clung on to both. They circled around me for a bit, and eventually rode off. Later I left a homemade card in a book in the self-help section in Islington library for someone to discover one day. I thought a lot about the person who tried to mug me, and what might be going on for them.

Day 271: I went to the dentist. The receptionist said, 'Miss Russell? The hygienist isn't here. I'm afraid there's been a boo-boo.' I laughed and said, 'You saying "boo-boo" has made it all better.' She said, 'To tell you the truth, I'm fed up.' Then she drew a smiley face on my appointment card. I left, and came back a bit later to give her a bag of Maltesers. I know this is slightly inappropriate for a dentist. She shouted, 'You are lovely!' as I left, a bit embarrassed.

Day 276: Last year I left a fiver on a number 47 bus going towards Lewisham. I had written on it, 'Have a treat on me' and signed it. Today a man from Nottingham messaged me on Twitter to say he had received the same note in change. Amazing!

Conversations on Kindness

This month began with me trying and failing to give blood. I was taking Gareth's advice seriously, looking for ways of being kind that didn't cost any money, and had made an appointment at the Surrey Quays mobile blood unit. I am the most squeamish person in the world, so I had set myself this task as a personal challenge. I was inspired by my little sister Kimberley, who has given so much blood over the years she has received a trophy. So off I went. Once I was there, I panicked in the extremely claustrophobic atmosphere of the mobile unit, failed to give blood and then ran away.

On the bus on the way home, feeling embarrassed and relieved in equal measure, I spotted a lady with her son, his arm in a grubby sling, asking if they could get on the bus for free. I could smell alcohol on her, even from three seats away. It was 10 a.m. She was trying and failing to get a special pass from the bus driver. I paid for them instead.

It had been a bit of an emotional start to the day. I had been musing philosophically that whoever crossed my path at any moment may have been there because there was something I could help them with, or something I could learn from our interaction. It was a kind of mythical way of looking at things, and interesting. But that morning I felt I had failed somehow. I didn't think I'd done as much as I could for the woman on the bus. I wished I'd had time to chat with her more, if she'd been up for that.

And the failure to give blood had bothered me. I knew that people give away far more than a measly pint of blood. In her book *The Keys to Kindness*, Claudia Hammond wrote about the incredible example of seventeen-year-old Abie who donated one of his kidneys to save the life of a stranger. I couldn't imagine doing that. I was beginning to learn a little about my limitations. When I got home, I tried to think of ways I could be kind for free without donating my organs.

Later that day, I met a very friendly man outside the tube station, collecting money for veterans. I gave him the change I had in my purse,

Compliment Slips

and he thanked me. When I asked if I could take his photograph, he joked that he would break my camera. I told him he was handsome, which made him blush and laugh. We had a nice long chat about what it's like collecting money for charity (hard work, he said, but on the whole people are 'very generous'). That interaction got me thinking, *I don't give enough compliments. They're effective, and they don't cost anything.*

Eureka! I'd got it! I can give people compliments. Since then, I have investigated the positive effects of paying strangers compliments, and they are impressive. In 2022 psychologists Vanessa Bohns and Erica Boothby from Cornell University in New York published the results of a study they had devised, in which they recruited volunteers who were given a simple task: to go up to a stranger of the same gender and compliment them by saying, 'I like your shirt.'

They asked the volunteers to record their thoughts about how good this compliment would make the other person feel. The volunteers were given an envelope to hand to the recipient of the compliment which contained a survey asking them to describe how good the compliment had made them feel, which they were then to place in a sealed envelope, to encourage them to be honest in their response. The strangers who received the compliments overwhelmingly reported that they had made them feel 'flattered' and 'good' – much more so than the volunteers had expected. One of the survey's other findings was that 'compliments also improve the mood of the compliment giver'.

So that month I tried to do a whole week of compliments. It seemed like a win-win situation. Also, I'd had a lot of practice by now at talking to strangers, so I wasn't too daunted. I told a woman in the ticket office at the National Film Theatre, who had admitted to me that she was exhausted, that she didn't look tired at all but looked like a 'magic pixie'. I told a man I sat next to on the number 47 bus that his eyes were like 'brown diamonds', which really intrigued him. We had a chat about whether brown diamonds actually existed. I told the staff in Starbucks in Brighton that they were all 'so funny and nice' that they should all be 'living lives of endless fun', which they loved. I told a woman on Lewisham High Street, 'Your trousers have cheered me up – they are the trousers of spring.' I told a waiter how nice and good at his job he was. I told a woman at Waterloo Station who was wearing extremely high shoes how elegant she looked. I told another lady she had amazing eyes and she said, 'Thanks. They're hereditary.' I said, 'Inherited from an angel. Oh no, sorry, that was a bit weird' and she said, 'No, I like weird. Weird is better than boring. You've cheered me up. I was really bored and now I'm not. I'm going to pay someone a compliment tomorrow. I might find a husband.'

During this period of intensive compliment-giving, I received two hugs and a KitKat from total strangers and had many long conversations with them too.

Once I had given compliments a few times, I gained confidence. I even eventually stood on a box opposite the Theatre Royal during the Brighton Festival in 2014 and gave people compliments as they passed by, the kind of thing you can get away with at a festival. I wrote the compliments on large pieces of card and handed them to strangers, as well as just calling out over a loudspeaker. It was fun.

But by mid-month, I was absolutely worn out. My sleep was erratic, I wasn't getting any spare time, I was spending more meaningful time with strangers than with my close friends and family. As for time for myself, well, there was none. As I got more and more tired, my inner critic really went to town on me, and my exhaustion meant I just didn't have the strength or inner resources to combat it with any positives. I was unfit and eating rubbish.

I realised that I should probably take better care of myself. I wanted to pass on what I had learned in an encouraging way, and I wanted to be a good ambassador for kindness. I wondered why I found being kind to myself so hard. Dr Kristin Neff, a pioneering researcher and teacher of self-compassion, and the co-founder of the Center for Mindful Self-Compassion, says that 'the biggest reason people aren't more self-compassionate is that they are afraid they'll become self-indulgent. They believe self-criticism is what keeps them in line. Most people have gotten it wrong because our culture says being hard on yourself is the way to be.'

I was very struck by something else I read in her book, *Self-Compassion: The Proven Power of Being Kind to Yourself*: 'No matter how hard we try, our best isn't good enough.'

Mm. That sounded very familiar.

I had never bothered with any of that self-care stuff, even though I had heard people extolling its virtues. I rebelled against it for years. I thought to myself, *Well, when the world is literally on fire, then damn right you should be doing everything you can at every moment to put the fire out and that doesn't involve self-indulgent bubble baths.* Harsh, I know. It's just I didn't think I had time to look after myself. I had persistently and pigheadedly resisted even thinking about it, and it wasn't until I got a very bad flu *twice* that month, that I began to consider being kind to myself as a priority. This began in small ways, allowing myself to rest when I was tired, making sure I had tasty and nutritious food to eat, going for walks in the woods when I felt jangled with stress.

Since then, one of the people from whom I have learned a great deal is Vicky Johnson, the founder and co-director of the Museum of Happiness in London. The MoH is a not-for-profit social enterprise that shares the art and science of sustainable happiness with individuals, communities, schools and organisations. It bases its work on research-backed positive psychology, focusing on mindfulness, self-compassion, gratitude and selfcare.

Vicky is a coach, resilience mentor and former youth worker. I spoke with her about her work, and the best tools to use to be kind to yourself.

Return to Love
with Vicky Johnson

I know you have helped many people learn how to be kinder to themselves, and happier, from starting out as a youth worker to your work with the Museum of Happiness. How did this journey begin for you?

I was a youth worker for seven years, and what really struck me at that time was the poor levels of mental health, self-love and self-kindness among the young people. We brought together young people from real pockets of deprivation, who were getting involved with gangs, and young people in care, and then other young people who were at private schools, from completely different backgrounds, and we mixed them all together. And it really broke down barriers. We got them to volunteer in their local communities, and they were making a positive contribution. Those who were getting themselves into gangs, and into trouble, they had this new community, this new support network, and they found out that it feels good to give and to be kind and to receive a 'positive feedback loop' for doing that. From that work I sensed there was something in this kind of work: in gratitude practice, focusing on kindness and being friends with your mind, so that's why I started the Museum of Happiness.

Why do you think that some of us find it so hard to be kind to ourselves?

Well, the brain has a natural negativity[1] bias, so we internalise a lot of those negative thoughts and ideas. And so now we have this distorted relationship with ourselves because of an unhelpful critical dialogue that we are in with ourselves. So, unless we retrain our brains with exercises

---

[1] Our tendency to pay more attention to negative experiences or information than to positive ones. Because our ancestors were constantly being exposed to threats, it's assumed that this was developed as an adaptive evolutionary function, to ensure their survival.

Compliment Slips

around self-compassion and positive psychology, we can get stuck in negative thinking. If you are one of those lucky people who was born into a family where they were showered with unconditional love, then you might not have the same kind of critical dialogue with yourself. But I think for a lot of people, their needs aren't met as a child, and it is not necessarily anyone's fault that this is the case. It's just that often parents have gone through trauma themselves, so they don't really have the love to give, or whatever it is that the young people need. So we may grow up feeling unloved, and there's a whole load of things at play, but I think that at the core, the negativity bias can play a part in why we don't feel love, and we operate from a place of fear and negativity.

And, as I learned from Dr Kristin Neff, the culture that we live in supports fear.

Yes, it does. So, when you think of the news and newspapers, they portray the world to be this awful scary place. Fred Rogers, who was a very influential American television host, said, 'When I was a boy and I would see scary things in the news, my mother would say to me, "Look for the helpers. You will always find people who are helping."' And they are always there. But that's not what is shown on mainstream media, we are shown all the fearful things, and told that the world is an awful place, so we are living our lives in a place of fear.

Our brains have three emotional regulation systems. We have our threat system, which spots all the threats; our drive system, which motivates us; and our soothe system to help us feel calm and relaxed. All mammals have this. But we're often living in our threat zone, so we perceive dangers which are probably not real, and we're in survival mode. In that position I think it's easy to disconnect from love: love for ourselves, love for others, love for the world, because the messages are 'Don't trust, be fearful.' For example, if someone does something kind for you in the street, you might be suspicious and wonder what they want, you might even see it as a threat. But when people can welcome the kindness, it's amazing! A lot of the work and my own personal journey have been about noticing when I have fallen into a place of fear, and then returning to love.

What would you say to someone who is new to all these ideas about how they could return to love, and be kind to themselves?

Firstly, if you are not feeling very good, notice that. Check in with your inner chatter, and ask yourself what type of thing am I saying to myself right now? Is it negative? Is it harsh? Is it critical? Our thoughts affect our emotions, so do check in and question the things you are saying to yourself. Ask yourself, 'Is this helpful? Would I say this to a good friend? Is there something kind I can say or do for myself right now?' And then tell yourself this: 'I'm doing the best I can right now, and that's all I can do, and that is enough.'

Remind yourself, tell yourself, that you are safe, that you are loved, that everything's going to be okay, so that you are being that voice of compassion, love and wisdom for yourself. We desire that so much for others, that they can be happy and not suffer. So, when we ourselves are going through a difficult time, we can feel like we want someone to scoop us up and say, 'You are loved, you are enough.' But that makes you quite dependent on others, and we want to be able to comfort ourselves. So that's kind of a starting point, to have that conversation with yourself.

Yes, and it takes some practice, I think, noticing when you are talking harshly to yourself, and countering that with self-kindness.

There are some things that I do that really help. A big part of my journey is prayer, and if prayer feels right, it's a great thing to do. It can be to whatever feels of resonance to you. For me, it started as praying to the universe, and now it's God and the universe. Prayer can be about us asking for help and guidance, if we are feeling afraid or feeling sad. At these moments I call in support from a higher power and ask for help to return to a place of love.

Another thing is just going for a walk in nature, without your phone or anything digital, to be able to go and connect to the magic of life. Nature is not giving you something and asking for something in return, it's not a transactional thing, Nature is giving with love and abundance. You know the sun rises every day, the birds are singing, there's all the beautiful flowers, and I think it's easy to forget that we are living in a miracle, the way everything operates, the intricate details, how everything is connected.

So, they would be my 'go to' things, to be kind to myself. Jon Kabat-Zinn [a renowned expert in stress reduction and mindfulness] says, 'You can't stop the waves, but you can learn to surf.' You know crazy things happen in the world, we live in a volatile, uncertain and complex world, we always have and maybe we always will, so how do we best take care of ourselves, how do we be the love we want to see in the world? It must start with our relationship with ourselves.

There was a time where I was doing so many kind things for others, but I was being horrible to myself. In my head I was saying, 'You stupid idiot, you should be able to cope with this.' For me that voice has now been trained to be a much kinder, supportive voice, my relationship with myself is kinder, it's more soothing, so I can really have my own back.

It's about the realisation that being kinder to yourself is a lifelong practice. If you wanted to become a weightlifter, you wouldn't think, 'I'll do loads of weight training for one day, and then I'll be done!' So, it's not 'I'll pray once and it will change things.' It's that there are ongoing practices which you can commit to, which will help you change your life forever.

Yes. It's these tiny little practices every day, so small that even on days with low motivation you can do it. For a long time I had 'I am enough' written on the mirror, and 'Be beautiful, be yourself', so that every day, when I look in the mirror, I see those words. For many years I had a really awful relationship with myself, with an eating disorder and all sorts of things, and it was these tiny little things, the moment-by-moment choices to be able to look in the mirror and see a positive message, even if I didn't agree with it straight away.

But the other kind of message, that you are not good enough as you are, is everywhere. Marketeers and brands and adverts are constantly trying to sell us things that we have so much of in a capitalist society. If we are trapped in fear, we're easier to control and manipulate, and what can keep us in fear is the message that you are not good enough as you are, so buy this product or service and then you'll be good enough. But we know that it doesn't work like that, we know we can't buy ourselves love, or buy ourselves sustainable happiness. We know it must come from within, and we can do it with these tiny little habits each day. So always ask yourself is there something kind I can do or say for myself right now?

Yes, I have adopted that, and it is incredibly powerful. I say it to myself at least a couple of times a day now!

Well, the brain responds to repetition. You'll find I say the same ten things in every session I teach, every day with everybody, because the repetition works.

I have also noticed how sometimes happiness and kindness are ideas that are criticised for being a bit wishy washy. One of the tools or mechanisms to combat that is science, and I think you hold both the art and science of happiness so well in your teachings. Is it useful for you to include the science?

A hundred per cent yes! I think by sharing the science it does help to persuade us of the power of kindness and happiness. It helps with the cynical part of our brains which might start to put up barriers. People love science and evidence-based research, like the work of Dr David

Compliment Slips

Hamilton [whom I mentioned in the last chapter], who has done so much research around the science of kindness, proving that it is literally contagious, and how kindness is the superpower of human beings. His research has proven that when you do something kind for someone, it releases all the happy hormones in your brain, the recipient's brain *and* the observer's brain! It's so incredible. Kindness is one of the only things that releases all the happy hormones.

I know you say you teach on a 'head, heart, hands' model. Could you explain that?

So, the head part is when we teach a little bit of theory and science, so that the brain can relax and say, 'I'll put down my walls of scepticism, I'll let it in a little bit.' The head part is about imparting scientific knowledge. But then scientific theory alone only gets us so far. The heart part is about values and appreciation, where we feel the power of it for ourselves.

And that might be by sharing stories of kindness and real-life examples?

Yes, so it's not just theory – we must feel it, we must understand it on a cellular level. And the hands part is okay, go forth and go do it, go practise!

So that could be, for example, being given kindness activities to try out?

Yes, because just knowing something is not going to change the world. You can have a driver's licence and not be a good driver, you could have great running shoes but unless you go out running it is not going to make a difference to your life. So I think we have to take charge, go forth and do those things we care about to make a difference. Don't think, 'Someone else will do it' or 'I'm too small to make a difference.' I think we have to be the love we want to see in the world.

I know you have a tattoo on your arm which says, 'I vow to live this day with love.' Could you speak about that?

I was at Thich Nhat Hanh's monastery [in India] this time last year, and there was an elderly nun there, and she'd lived through the Vietnam War. She said that she knew that there were bombs falling from the sky, knew that people were suffering and dying, and that if she disconnected from love and went into a place of fear and despair, she couldn't serve herself, or anybody, that she would be stuck and trapped in fear. She said she realised that there was so much fearful energy in the world right now that she needed to be this force of love. She sang, 'How can I heal a wounded heart if I can only see the dark? I vow this day to live with love, whatever is happening, I vow to live this day with love.'

It's so powerful, so I thought if in six months, on my birthday, I still feel so strongly about this message, and I had an inkling that I would, I'll have a tattoo, and hopefully when I'm a hundred-year-old lady and looking back at my life I hope I can look at this and say, 'I tried my best to live each day with love.'

And people often ask me, what have you got written on your arm? If I'm in a coffee shop or in a meeting and even complete strangers ask about it, I tell them the story, and it's a really nice way to share the message.

Is there one self-kindness practice that has really blown your mind, or do you have a favourite?

Gratitude. Dr Robert Emmons, who is the world's leading scientific expert on gratitude, says that if, just before bedtime, you can invite your mind to reflect on three good things that happened that day, it releases oxytocin, the love and connection hormone, so you can sleep more easily, feel more optimistic and see the good in your life.

Compliment Slips

If you do that every day for about six to eight weeks, the neurons in your brain will form a different pathway, so instead of asking, 'What's wrong?' your brain will ask, 'What's right?' If you can start to see the good and the blessings you have in your life, it changes everything. Even on the day that we got burgled at the Museum of Happiness, because I had been doing the gratitude practice for quite a while, I walked in and thought about all the things that hadn't been taken instead of all the things that had, and I realised it had changed my brain.

There's a quote I love from [American historian] Alice Morse Earle which exemplifies this: 'Every day might not be good. But there is something good in every day.' And I have found that it is the most accessible exercise for people as well. We've done this with elderly people, with four-year-olds, with people experiencing homelessness, with city bankers, you know, everybody. Despite any suffering they might be going through, everyone has managed to find something to be grateful for. So gratitude would be my top tip. It's so simple and so beautiful, and it has the biggest impact and, hand on heart, and I wouldn't say this lightly, if you do this practice, it will change your life.

This was the month I learned that you can't, as the saying goes, 'pour from an empty cup'. I found some teachers, both online and in real life. I read some books about being kind to yourself, and I learned to meditate. Later, through joining Vicky's Museum of Happiness community, I began to build a toolbox of things to comfort and support me when I was down on myself, including gratitude practice. I began to give myself the love and compassion that I gave to others.

I even tried – and it was pretty cringey, to be honest – to pay myself compliments! And in doing so I realised how often I insult myself. This is a common habit, I know, something so many of us do. We criticise ourselves and our lives and thus reduce the joy of the everyday. Our harsh inner critic can diminish the things we are good at, the pleasures we have, the beauty and wonder of the moment, all the things we deserve to allow ourselves to enjoy. The journey of learning to be kind to myself is still one I am travelling on and was harder by far than the journey to learn to be kind at every opportunity to anyone and everyone who crosses my path. But it is so important.

11. JUNE

Amazing Grace

> *Five acts of kindness this month:*
>
> **Day 291:** We were asked to put on a royal-themed storytelling event as part of the Alternative Village Fete in Battersea Park. I gave away loads of sweets, paper crowns, homemade cakes and strawberries to kids in the park – it was quite expensive to buy food in there, so we were pretty popular.
>
> **Day 296:** I discovered that a lovely man on the reception at Birmingham Rep was celebrating his birthday, so I bought him cake.
>
> **Day 298:** I helped a woman buy a travel card at Canada Water tube station. This was tricky, as she only spoke a little English and I don't speak any Spanish. But we managed with lots of very bad mime and laughter.
>
> **Day 306:** I gave a man with his arm in a sling a small gift. He said, 'Am I your act of kindness today?' This is the first time anyone asked me that. I wonder if he knows what I am up to?
>
> **Day 308:** I did half an hour of litter-collecting round Edgbaston Reservoir in Birmingham, after a woman told me her dog got poorly eating an old sack and I saw a jogger stumble over a discarded inhaler. Collected a big bag full.

Despite all this learning and joy, there was no denying that I was still holding on to a lot of pain, and I became acutely aware of this. I wondered if the source of it might be what author and psychologist Dr Sharon Blackie refers to as the 'father wound'. Dr Blackie writes about how many psychologists suggest that this harm inflicted by our fathers can impact our self-image, self-worth and confidence, so that we feel we are never good enough. This sounded familiar. Yes, I did notice how often I told myself I was bound for failure and rejection, as I had discovered and begun to deal with in May. But I knew that if I wanted to be kind to myself as well, and I had accepted that this was important, then I had to try to do some healing with both of my dads – my biological father who abandoned me and my sister, and my stepdad who inflicted so much harm on my whole family. Honestly, the prospect of each of these was terrifying; both seemed almost insurmountable.

But I had met so many strangers already that year, and the one thing I had learned was the truth in that saying I mentioned earlier: 'Everyone is fighting a battle you know nothing about.' Perhaps this also applied to my dads.

I dealt with the easier of the two dad dilemmas first. Many years earlier, my sister and I had tried to reach out to our dad with the help of the Salvation Army. Our uncle, my biological dad's brother, had responded and regretfully informed us that our dad had said he didn't want to be in touch, so that was that. We found out at that time that we had three half-brothers. We exchanged Christmas cards with Dad after this, but that had been the extent of our contact.

Now I began to write to him sometimes, just to say hello – kind letters, light-hearted. From his side, the Christmas cards kept coming.

My stepdad Terry was more of a challenge. I did consider visiting him, as I knew where he lived. I thought about giving him the chance to say sorry, even of hearing his story. But in the end the kinder thing to do for myself was to stay away. For years he'd denied any wrongdoing on his part, called us liars, and it was too great an emotional risk for me to allow the possibility of that happening again.

I recalled the other Terry, the homeless man I met in Soho, and his profound unhappiness. I sometimes heard snippets of my stepdad's life, and it sounded sad and lonely too. My life was full and happy. But still, I just didn't know how to forgive him, and so it was hard to let go of anger and pain. I started to get curious about forgiveness, to wonder how people found it in their hearts to forgive, and what good it did them.

I eventually came across The Forgiveness Project on LinkedIn. I signed up for a training course they were running online, which was all about 'working with stories of lived experience'. Afterwards, I reached out to the founder, Marina Cantacuzino, in the hope of learning more about the power and possibilities of forgiveness from this amazing author, broadcaster and award-winning journalist.

The F Word
with Marina Cantacuzino

Could I ask you firstly how The Forgiveness Project started?

I was a jobbing freelance journalist feature writer in 2003, during the lead-up to the protest against the Iraq War in Hyde Park. I often say the project grew out of anger; although I am not a particularly angry person, I was infuriated then.

That march politicised me, and I thought, *What, as a journalist, can I do?* Well, the only thing I could do was collect stories which could give a different narrative to the one of revenge and retaliation. So to begin with it was a private project done in my spare time with a photographer friend.

We were travelling for work and when we weren't doing the assignment, we looked for stories from victims and survivors who had suffered atrocity and harm, and who had sought peaceful solutions. And stories from perpetrators who transformed their aggression into a force for peace. I didn't know the term restorative justice at that point, but it was a restorative project because it was looking at both sides of the story, and these were very journalistic, informed first-person narratives, with strong photographic portraits.

Conversations on Kindness

This eventually became an exhibition called 'The F Word' which we launched in the Oxo Gallery, London. It was phenomenally successful, and I was completely bowled over, to be honest with you. I hadn't expected it at all. People were saying, 'You must do more with these stories.' We had collected twenty-six of them by now, from all over the world. Then we managed to get some funding from Anita Roddick [founder of The Body Shop and a renowned human- and animal-rights campaigner] to bring twelve of the storytellers over to London. The launch went on for two days, and the people who came, victims and perpetrators, told us that we had created an incredibly healing space. So, on the back of that, I founded The Forgiveness Project, which has storytelling at its heart, and it's my attempt to change the narrative.

And what is it you are looking for in these stories?

I am seeking out evidence of people who have made meaning out of their trauma. One of our storytellers calls herself a story healer, which I like. I suppose it's the wounded healer kind of concept.

Yes, I like that too. Can I ask why you think it's important to tell stories of trauma healing?

I know as a journalist that stories stick, they have a profound impact on people – it's the only way to build empathy and connection. Facts don't do it, experts can say motivational things and you think, 'Amazing', but if you read, watch, listen, one to one, hear the story of the other, it builds understanding. You walk into their world. We can easily connect with people like us; the difficult thing is to connect with people not like us, to experience what they're experiencing, perhaps in a different continent, and here I am talking about continent in a metaphorical as well as a literal way.

We must hear the stories and then the conversation starts. If you can't have the dialogue with the actual person whose stories you're being exposed to, you can at least have it with others, and your perspective changes. Everything is about perspective change, I think, as we can get locked into a rigid way of thinking.

In the introduction to one of your books you wrote, 'We are creating the opportunity for people to choose forgiveness and we're presenting it as a resilient response to hurt and trauma.' Would you say that's one of the main benefits of reading your book or listening to the F Word podcast?

It doesn't even have to go that deep, it can be literally just a light-bulb moment of understanding. As one of our ex-offenders once said, it's the head-to-heart transition. I have had people contact me over the years who have told me that they never expected to be so profoundly impacted by reading this or coming to hear so-and-so speak, but that it really made them think differently, and helped them process some of what happened to them. A woman who came to that initial exhibition wrote in the visitor's book, 'Now I want to meet the person who attacked me' – you know, it inspired her to look at the trauma, and another woman said, 'Telling my story saved me from it.'

Certainly, for me it felt like a gentle invitation to understand that considering painful things can be cathartic or healing. The connection for me with kindness was around forgiving myself and those who harmed me. Forgiveness feels like an act of compassion and self-compassion in the same moment. Desmond Tutu said in the foreword to your book, 'All of us have the capacity to arise to a generosity of spirit that can transform the world, to forgive is not just to be altruistic, in my view it's the best form of self-interest.' That feels truthful to me. I wondered if for you there is a connection between compassion, self-compassion and forgiveness?

I think we like to see ourselves mostly as morally deeply sound people, and so when we're not, it kind of exacerbates self-destructive feelings and behaviour. That's why I think self-compassion and self-forgiveness and kindness to ourselves are so important in this world. if you are very upset with yourself, it can take over your life at its most extreme, if it's what you go to bed thinking about, wake up in the morning thinking about, and it affects everything. So self-compassion allows you to get out of the way of yourself, and by doing that you can be compassionate to others, open up, be forgiving to those that harmed you.

Sandra Barefoot from the prison project RESTORE [who I met in Chapter 8] *said maybe radical compassion is sometimes saying this person needs to be kept away from everyone else because they'll hurt people and because they want to be kept away. But the spaces we put those people in should be kind. Do you agree?*

Well, for me, it's quite clear that some people need to remain in prison for the rest of their lives, because they will just create too much damage when they come out. But most people can be rehabilitated. I do believe in the possibility of a form of redemption, for most people. Some people I think are so damaged, whether that's to do with their wiring in their brain, or to do with their background and their trauma, and those two things are connected, I think it's very hard in some cases to see any change.

You know there's the Zulu idea of *ubuntu*, that we are all inherently connected, just inextricably linked to each other, so you can't just write off someone as a monster. Samantha Lawler, one of The Forgiveness Project's storytellers, whose mother was murdered by her father, talks about forgiveness not being about forgiving the act or the person, but about forgiving the imperfection of humanity, which is in all of us, so forgiveness becomes a greater thing; it's forgiving humanity for being flawed.

Yes, that is a truly deep and profound kind of forgiveness. And perhaps being forgiven can help some people to transform?

Yes. Another of our storytellers is an American man called Arno Michaelis who had been deeply involved in the White Power movement. He changed his ways because of the kindness of others, because the people he hated the most showed him the most kindness. One day he went into a McDonald's, and he's got swastikas tattooed all over his fingers, and the woman behind the counter, a black woman, said, 'You are better than that' and it was a key moment of transformation for him. He also spoke about his co-workers being Latinos, who he hated, and gay people, who he also hated. Many of them didn't return the hate he put out, and their acts of kindness transformed him, so it has an impact, somehow: with kindness, hate and anger, everything melts away.

That made me think about my sweatshirt which says, 'Kindness is Magic' and when I wear it people sometimes ask me, 'What do you mean by magic?'

Because it is alchemy.

Yes, it's an alchemical process that transforms people. And forgiveness is that, too. They feel like things you can cling onto if you find yourself in choppy emotional waters, they can pull you out, or keep you afloat.

Definitely. A very clear good example of that is Figen Murray. Her son was killed in the Manchester Arena bombings in 2017. Two weeks after the bombings, as she was just coming out of the terrible, terrible shock and beginning to process the trauma, she saw on television what happened following an attack on Muslims in Finsbury Park. She saw Imam Mohammed Mahmoud putting a protective circle around Darren Osborne, the man who tried to kill them.

She was so moved by that image, that she suddenly realised that, like the imam, she had to demonstrate the very values that were so lacking when her son died – values of kindness, compassion and forgiveness – and she said that that's what has allowed her to stay within her humanity and it's been her life's work ever since.

Do you think there are any limitations on forgiveness as a healing tool?

Well, there's been some research into abusive relationships, where there has been domestic violence, and research shows, perhaps unsurprisingly, that (in those cases) the more you forgive, the kinder you are to the person who is harming you, the more that harm will continue. I think if Desmond Tutu was here now, he would say that doesn't preclude forgiveness, though. But don't be a masochist: you can forgive and release. You can forgive but get out of harm's way, and therefore release yourself as well.

Yes, you can get into 'What is the definition of kindness in this situation?' Am I being kind to myself right now? Am I going to step away from you while you are being violent? And am I being kinder to you in fact if I say, 'No, this is not how you behave, this is not acceptable'?

Yes, it's tough love, isn't it? It's what parents must do to children who become addicted. This is what we mean when we say 'be cruel to be kind'.

So, if you're stuck, if something or someone is hurting you, then you must be kind first to yourself.

Yes. Also, regarding forgiveness, in my most recent book, *Forgiveness: An Exploration*, I write about a woman who was a victim of sexual assault and even though she says she totally understands the benefits of forgiving and would be up for it, she says she will not give that as a gift, because she is in solidarity with all women who've been sexually abused, therefore she doesn't in any way want to imply that all abusers should be forgiven. It's a solidarity, community thing for her. Which I think is quite interesting.

So what can we all do to help make a less vengeful and kinder world?

Amazing Grace

One thing we can do is to be kind on social media, which is a lot more productive than to snipe, because one can just sink into stereotypes and amplify things that are unhelpful. It is interesting to either ignore attacks or, if you are going to respond, don't do it critically. Thank people for what they've done or said, find a different and kinder way of communicating.

I really believe that even in social media spaces, even when they seem toxic, there is more good than bad, more hope than fear, more light than dark. And more kindness, online and in the real world.

I think you are right. It's like when you ask someone in the street for help, people go out of their way, don't they?

They do. I see that, every day. So it is about allowing yourself to see it. Online and offline.

Forgiveness felt like the ultimate challenge and opportunity for me. I had learned that it could set you free. It's a way of being kind to yourself by allowing yourself to heal, letting go of anger and pain, and it is a way of being kind to the person or persons you forgive. And I thought, *Lots of people have forgiven far more quickly than me and forgiven much worse things, too.* I also thought, *I am doing my best.* This is difficult to think about. But I will try. I will try. As for both my dads, well, I wanted to forgive them both, and I started by accepting that I didn't know anything about their sufferings, their disappointments or their fears.

Around about the time I found enough courage to write to my stepdad, I discovered that he had died. Still, I wrote to him. It's a letter I wish I had written sooner, but it felt like a powerful thing to do. Here it is:

Conversations on Kindness

Dear Terry,

What can I do, now that you are dead and I can't knock on your door and say we need to talk, in the way I have imagined so many times? Truthfully, what I wanted from you, and from my birth father too, was for you to make that move, to approach me, but I waited too long for that impossible wish to come true. So all I am left with now really is the option to write to you, the letter I didn't write to you when you were alive. To tell you how your abuse left me with a deep sense of unworthiness which lasted for many years.

I am writing to you also because I want to forgive you, and now I have to find a way to do that knowing that the possibility of you asking my forgiveness or saying sorry is now gone forever. Somehow, to be kind to myself, I have to forgive you anyway. I have learned a lot about forgiveness in the past few years: that it is powerful and can help release a lot of pain and anger.

It's a tall order, to ask yourself to forgive the person who caused so much damage to you when you were such a small child and so vulnerable. And the person who caused so much damage to the people you love most in the world.

But I do not know the pain you carried. I really wish we had found time to talk and the courage to be honest.

I want you to know that all I wanted was a dad to do 'dad things' with, someone to teach me stuff, and to play games with, and to explain things I didn't understand, to tell me stories and to protect and look after me. I'm sorry for both of us that didn't happen.

I wish you had found the courage to say sorry to me and I really think that would have been such a powerful experience for you. I have some inkling of what you suffered at your own father's hands. So I wish that we could have sat in each other's

Amazing Grace

company and that suffering, pain, guilt, anger, remorse, all those things could have been expressed and could have been exorcised. So that you could have forgiven yourself too. I hope you found some peace at the end.

Also, I want to let you know that I have always sought light and kindness in hope in the world and in everyone in it, because of the darkness I saw. So in a strange way, that longing to find the good in the world, I owe to you. I have grasped life and all its adventure with all my might, too. I don't think that you did that, and I am sorry that you were not able to.

So I forgive you, and I forgive myself. I forgive all of us human beings for being flawed, and for the pain we cause each other. I vow to seek the light and to be grateful for the many gifts I have and to be kind, to myself, to others, to the whole world, always.

Bernadette

I believe Terry died a very unhappy man, ill and obese in a small flat with few friends to comfort him. This made me sad. After I wrote the letter I burned it on Southsea beach, near where I used to live. I imagined breathing it out, the hurt, the rage. I felt deep relief and peace in that moment. I said goodbye to him. I went home.

I thought of the gratitude practice that Vicky Johnson taught me, and how I have so much to be grateful for: my partner, my lovely family, my loyal friends, an interesting and rich life, a safe home. I remembered that my kindness journey had started with a huge tragedy: the needless death of a young man whose family and friends still mourn him. And I am alive. Alive in a wonderful, beautiful, complex world. So forgiveness was the deepest and most profound kindness I could do for myself.

I don't mind carrying a scar from my childhood – we all bear scars. But scars and wounds are different. Scars are places of healing – they remind us of what we have survived. Wounds are places of pain where the suffering remains present. I thought about what Marina Cantacuzino said, about the 'wounded healer' concept, a term coined by psychotherapist Carl Jung in 1951. The idea that someone may want to heal others because they themselves are wounded. But I thought I'd rather be a scarred healer, not a still wounded one.

And so I began work on forgiving myself. For the things I did and chose when I was just trying to survive. For passing up opportunities because of lack of confidence, for not looking after myself as well as I could have, for not spending enough time with the people I love, for the things I wanted and pursued that weren't very good for me, for spending time on things that made me unhappy, for pretending to be okay when I wasn't, for not listening better, for not working on forgiveness sooner, for being a flawed human being. I'm a work in progress. But it has helped, so much. I hope, if this impacts you too, that you can also forgive yourself.

During this month of deep soul-searching, I really enjoyed playful acts of kindness, too. On what I knew was my neighbour's birthday I decorated the path to his door with chalked poetry and little gifts and flowers, for him to discover on his way to work. I rang a stranger and sang them 'Happy Birthday', as requested by someone via Twitter. I gave books to our community library. I continued to notice all the daily acts of kindness that keep the darkness at bay.

I had found something that would never fail me.

12. JULY

Journey's End

Five acts of kindness this month:

Day 319: At the Whitechapel interchange for the Overground line, I saw a woman struggling with her buggy, hurrying to get a train. At the bottom was a tiny boy with his lip trembling. I scooped him up and carried to his mum and they made the train – I was like a friendly child catcher.

Day 322: I gave my friend's grandad a ukulele lesson – he had wanted to learn for a long time and is a George Formby fan! Great fun.

Day 331: At our storytelling show I found out it was a woman's birthday. I got everyone to sing 'Happy Birthday' to her and cobbled together a present and card.

Day 333: Today, my Oyster card slipped out of its folder and fell onto the tracks as I was getting off the tube. I had to explain myself to the guard, and was expecting trouble.

Him: That is bad luck.
Me: I know!
Him: Go through.
Me: Really?
Him: Yes. You can't have more bad luck.
Me: You are the nicest underground staff person; you are absolutely the best one. Plus, you have a smile like a ray of sunshine.
Him (*laughs*): Oh my God!
His colleague: Oy! I heard that! What about me?!
Me: And you. You both are. I'd like to give you a reward, but I don't have one.
Him: You can get us a coffee tomorrow.
Me: Okay.

Day 334: I went to the charity shop in Highgate. I left a little note inside one of the second-hand bags, saying, 'This is a magic bag, every time you use it you will have an extremely lucky day' and I put a pound in it.

Conversations on Kindness

The lead-up to the 2012 Summer Olympics had begun, and that year London was hosting. The opening ceremony was on the evening of 27 July. In a statement about the event, director Danny Boyle said, 'We hope . . . that through all the noise and excitement . . . you will glimpse a single golden thread of purpose – the idea of Jerusalem – of a better world, the world of real freedom and true equality . . . belief that we can build Jerusalem. And that it will be for everyone.' My brilliant friend the choreographer Natasha Khamjani had been headhunted to be an integral part of the 'mass movement team', which meant, among many other responsibilities, that she was asked to teach 80,000 audience members to move and participate in the pre-show ceremony. She told me how electrifying it was, to know that in that one moment – as the Olympic rings were forged and lifted as if on fire – millions of people were watching the same thing. It was humanity at its best, she said, working together, to deliver this beautiful, incredible, seemingly impossible thing. 'I looked up at those five rings in that heart-stopping moment and considered what they stood for: as they represent five inhabited continents of the world coming together, in harmony, unity and peace. It was incredible.'

I was immensely moved and inspired by the Olympics. It felt deeply symbolic, too: that the flaming of burning buildings I had seen at the beginning of this journey that had been so distressing for many, had been replaced by the flame of the Olympic torch, a symbol of hope and possibility, in this final month of my year of kindness.

Fire, which had destroyed so much a year earlier, was also the element that lit the darkness and showed us a way out of it. Gigantic viewing screens were being put up on the banks of the Thames and in parks and other outdoors spaces all over the UK, so people could come together and watch, for free. There was a carnival atmosphere, even on the tube. People were laughing and talking to each other more than usual and wearing silly hats. My sister and I managed to get tickets for a couple of

Journey's End

the Paralympic events and we were delighted. London was even more magical than usual, and everyone seemed to be smiling.

My acts of kindness and my interactions with strangers were getting more and more enchanting, strange and delightful too. I received many lovely messages this month via social media, including this, from a friend of a friend: 'I've never even met Bernadette Russell, but she still inspires me to be kinder. Thanks, love.' Plus, I continued to have some hilariously eccentric interactions in the streets as I chatted with random strangers. For example, I got talking to a man on the number 47 bus after offering him some chocolate. He told me he was a mathematician and used to be 'very good friends' with the Beach Boys. He spent the journey trying to teach me Esperanto, in which he claimed to be fluent. The journey passed very quickly. I met a woman called Cindy on Russell Street in Covent Garden, in a sweet shop called Hope and Glory. She told me she was loving the warm weather but was 'parched'. I went back later with a bottle of orange juice for her. She gave me a giant lollipop. That lollipop, in turn, provoked many other conversations as I wandered about licking it like a modern-day Willy Wonka. Then there was the time on the tube after a very long day that I met two women dressed as tigers, who were travelling home with their non-tiger friend. We had a chat:

Me: Where have you two cats been?
Tiger 1: Late night at London Zoo.
Me: You look amazing.
Tiger 2: Thanks.
Me: I know I'm not supposed to feed the animals, but would you accept a small gift? (*I had some biscuits.*)
Tiger 1: Er . . .
Tiger 2: Yes, please.
Non-tiger friend of the tigers: You've made them very happy.
Me: They've made me happy.

It was all making me happy. That month I began to decorate phone boxes, after deciding that they looked a bit woebegone and that it would be an 'act of community kindness' to jazz them up a bit. I snuck out at night, scrubbing and cleaning them until they gleamed (yes, this was a disgusting job, so let's not linger on it!), and then decorated them with paper bunting, balloons, poetry, inspirational quotes, jars of sweets and boxes of cakes.

I did that eight times, and pictures of the transformed phone boxes started to turn up on Twitter. A few people messaged me to say how much they had cheered them up. When I did the final one, opposite Crossfield's Estate in Deptford, a woman contacted me to say that she had seen the decorated phone box and gone in out of curiosity. That time I'd put a sign up which read, 'Phone someone you love', with a 50p piece stuck to it. She told me she'd phoned her boyfriend, whom she'd had an argument with the night before, and met him in the phone box, where they had made up. Nice.

Life was going to be boring, I started to think, when this year of kindness was over. I couldn't *really* remember what it had been like before, but I was pretty sure it hadn't been as interesting or uplifting. I could say I had one thing in common with the Olympic runners, and that was that there was a finish line in sight for me too. Would I carry on? Was this my 'life's work' now? And, if so, how exactly?

I was, in a very ramshackle and disorganised way, conducting research of a kind, without the scientific approach of careful data collection and analysis and peer-reviewed papers. Instead, I was doing it just by being in the world, by acting, observing, experimenting and recording the results via Facebook posts. But soon I was to meet many people who have dedicated themselves to researching as well as practising kindness in a much more professional and structured way. One of these people is the brilliant 'Professor of Kindness' himself, Robin Banerjee, previously Head of the School of Psychology and now Pro-Vice-Chancellor

Journey's End

for Global and Civic Engagement at the University of Sussex. Professor Banerjee also founded the Sussex Centre for Research on Kindness, which is dedicated to illuminating the nature of kindness and how it plays a role in people's wellbeing and in different aspects of society.

Recently, he has led a project called The Kindness Test (which I mentioned in Chapter 1), working in partnership with the award-winning broadcaster and writer Claudia Hammond, Visiting Professor for the Public Understanding of Psychology at the University of Sussex. The project was the biggest ever public science project on kindness. It was conducted by a team of researchers based at the University of Sussex, in partnership with BBC Radio 4.

How it worked was this: an anonymous survey was launched in 2021, aimed at helping the researchers 'learn more about how kindness is viewed within society at large' and exploring issues including: What are the most common kind acts people carry out? Where do people most often experience kindness? What are the barriers to behaving kindlier? How is kindness valued in the workplace? Is kindness viewed as a weakness? What prevents people from being kinder? How does kindness relate to factors such as wellbeing, mental health, geographical location, gender and personality? How is kindness connected with compassion and empathy? How does kindness relate to our value systems? The results were announced on BBC Radio 4 in March 2022, in a series called *The Anatomy of Kindness*.

Towards a Culture of Kindness
with Professor Robin Banerjee

I know that you are instrumental in the establishment of the kindness research at the University of Sussex, and I wanted to ask what made you decide on the subject?

Well, the work I was doing in psychology focused on education and mental health with children and teenagers, on their social and emotional competencies, how they get on with each other in the world, and how they navigate that social world Schools increasingly see the social and emotional development of children and young people as a core part of their school experience. So it's not just something that happens in the background or on the side.

And it really got me thinking that this is about fixing the environment, rather than fixing the child. And that's where the focus on kindness came in. We realised that the question we should be asking is, 'What would a kind school look like? What does a kind environment look like at school?' And when you ask those questions, it gives you a very different focus, because it's not just about encouraging or teaching children to be kind. It's about transforming an environment into one that nurtures kindness.

I started talking about creating a school that feels kind, not just for the children, but all the staff who work there, the visitors, the parents, the carers, the wider community. And then I started talking about this with other people, who said, it's the same in hospitals. It's the same in social work, in charity work, politics, law. You could be working in a bank, and you could ask the same question about how kind is this environment, right?

And that is where the whole interdisciplinary focus started to come in. I always felt like psychologists are only ever going to have a little part of the answer. You've got to work with people from all different disciplines to tackle big issues. And they were all saying they could look at what they're doing through the lens of kindness as well. Wherever we're working, we could be asking, 'Is this an environment that cultivates kindness? Could we do things differently to inspire kindness in that environment?' That really inspired me. And that's how the kindness research came to be.

Journey's End

I was fascinated by just how much academic interest there is and how much research is being conducted in this area now. Do you know why this is?

Well, we're still trying to make the case for kindness being a good subject for academic study and science, as the research is still very much in its infancy. And I'm still having to go out and say, 'This is something to be taken seriously, this is something that needs our attention', after having worked in this field for a long time.

But you're right that there is a real growth in this area. I don't think it's coming from science or from academia. I think it's coming from us as members of society, as members of the community, as people. And I think that's important. There's a lot of amazing research to draw on, which is great. But it hasn't been understood and framed in terms of kindness, and a lot of times when I'm working with researchers they say, yes, we do have some interesting results relating to that, we just haven't used the word 'kindness' before.

It's almost like there is a taboo around the word, or a resistance to using it.

I think a lot of it is because when they think about kindness, it just feels like something that's a bit soft and fluffy. But that's changing, you know. I think it's getting more attention now, because people are feeling a need for it in our world today, perhaps more than ever before.

What is a kindness culture?

I suppose it's a culture where kindness is valued, celebrated and cultivated. And I think it's a culture where kindness can grow, and that's not *despite* the culture, but grow *because* that is the culture. We do see a lot of kindness around us, and I'm happy to say that the world is a very kind place. When we did the BBC project The Kindness Test, it was really striking how ready people were to identify kindness as something that they had very recently experienced, so kindness is all around.

But sometimes, sadly, kindness happens despite the culture of a place, and I think moving towards a kindness culture could reverse that. Kindness culture is about saying kindness is happening, because we've got a supportive culture for it. And I think a lot of that comes down to valuing it and celebrating it, not just implicitly but explicitly saying it.

Did you find it hard to convince people of the importance of kindness in their organisations?

Yes, when I was first working in that area of promoting social and emotional skills in schools, I had to fight quite hard for people to take it seriously, because they were saying, 'Oh, we do all that. We're a very friendly place' or 'We're a very happy place.' And what we realised is that we need to be explicit about what we're doing to nurture kindness, and that we feel it's important.

If we don't, too many people assume it doesn't really count. If you don't have a kindness culture, people will think, well, it's a nice 'extra' to have, but it's not fundamental, not a core value. I do a lot of work now with people in different types of organisations, whether that's hospitals or businesses, as well as schools – and I think this is changing. I think a lot of people would say, kindness is 'nice', but we also must live in the real world, which is sort of tough, challenging and competitive. And we've got scarce resources, so we've got to be efficient and effective. And my point, what I keep banging on about, is that when you talk about kindness, value kindness, celebrate kindness, grow kindness, what you'll find is that that's not in opposition to all those other priorities.

Let's talk more about The Kindness Test. Could you give me a brief outline of it?

Fundamentally the aim was to shine a light on kindness. Let's talk about it. Let's notice it, let's celebrate it. Of course, there were also a lot of very specific questions that we wanted to answer in terms of the science of

Journey's End

kindness. It was a unique opportunity, working with the BBC and with Claudia Hammond. We started talking about doing a survey of kindness together, but we had to persuade the BBC commissioning editors that kindness would be a good topic.

At first, there was some concern around how much there was to say about kindness. I made the case that there was a lot to talk about! And that it was going to inspire and engage people. In the end, out of all the surveys that have been conducted with BBC Radio 4 and their various academic partnerships, The Kindness Test got the biggest response. We had over 60,000 people from around the world taking part in the survey.

I wonder whether that was connected to the time that it took place, because it was in the middle of lockdown?

I think it probably was related, because something interesting happened psychologically in the context of Covid. I think it made us all ask the question, 'What are the points of connection that really matter to us?' and I think that is a reason why kindness is important, because, in my opinion, kindness is all about connecting people.

Perhaps there was something about being disconnected in certain ways at that time which highlighted the importance of it.

Absolutely. Even though everybody had radically different Covid experiences, we all ended up being confronted by the same questions, about how we are connected to what's around us. With The Kindness Test, we found when we asked people, 'When was the last time you did something kind for someone else?' and then asked them about their feelings afterwards, there were lots of positive things. People rated feelings of happiness, pride, things like that. But the highest rating was given for feeling connected with each other, which I thought was interesting. So, there is something important about kindness and social connections in the broader sense.

When I set out on my own journey, I wanted to see if kindness could change the world. Do you think that kindness can make a meaningful, significant contribution to positive change in the world?

Absolutely. The fundamental thing that you're doing is bringing people together, so they are not isolated in facing challenges. It doesn't take away the challenges. You only need to open a newspaper to be aware of all the difficulties and problems in the world. So, I'm not suggesting that this is a silver bullet that's going to remove all the challenges in the world. But in a kindness culture we are facing them together.

One of the big questions for me is, who is the 'we'? Sometimes people take great issue with work on empathy, and to some extent kindness, because they say people are so selective. The idea is that it's very easy for us to be kind and empathic towards people who are thinking the same as us, or who have the same background as us, and the worry is that we can be kinder and more empathic, but only towards people like us. And my answer to that is always that's a very legitimate concern. And there's good evidence for it. But let's not use that to knock the whole concept of kindness.

Yes, I was aware of that early on in my journey. There's a little joke in my theatre show about kindness where I say, 'I thought I shouldn't be just kind to people who I like the look of — I should be kind to people that I don't like the look of.' I remember an occasion when I realised I was avoiding this man because he had such a loud voice, and I have a prejudice there, that people with loud voices are going to be rude and aggressive, which is of course unfair and daft. So I had a lovely conversation with him, and he was fantastic. If you keep noticing your own biases and not allowing them to influence your behaviour towards people, you don't miss out on meaningful connections with them.

Yes, and what we must do is ask ourselves: how do we get to a point where we're being genuinely generous in terms of expressing our kindness, communicating that empathy, towards everybody? So that is not just about people like me, or people who think the same as me. And that's hard. For me, for you, for everybody, I'm sure. It's an ongoing journey, but it doesn't mean that we should let go of it. It's more important than ever.

Do you think that the research you and your team conducted might persuade people to be kinder? Do you think statistics and studies have their own power to change minds? And how so?

Well, they really help with the task of shining a light on kindness. If we don't have the stories to share, it doesn't feel real, and it certainly doesn't feel important. So I think stories do speak to people. And we've got loads and loads of statistics, too. From the results of The Kindness Test, we can observe that seeing kindness, receiving kindness and giving kindness are each associated positively with wellbeing. Claudia's book contains all those little snippets of kindness, like people talking about the last time someone was kind to them, the last time they were kind to someone else, a hundred thousand little moments which are amazingly powerful. You realise that small act made a difference in that moment to that person, to the extent that they remember it. So stories very much bring to life the importance of kindness. The other side of it is around demonstrating why it makes sense to focus on a kindness culture and to make the case for it. When you've got all these pressures around resources and efficiency and getting things right and hitting your bottom-line targets and things like that, I think that's where data is incredibly helpful, and having good scientific research helps.

I was really fascinated to read that your work began in child psychology. I work in schools a lot, and I'm struck by how kindness is always a positive thing in primary schools. It's often literally written on the walls. It's voiced as a core value. It's sewn into teaching practice. But I've also noticed it often disappears as part of the conversation during secondary and further education. I was thinking about how that's weird messaging from us, in that it's almost like we say to secondary school children, you can stop being kind now because you need to get your GCSEs. And we adults aren't modelling kindness very well either in terms of political landscape and leadership, and yet we do seem to expect it from children. Has that been your experience?

That has been my experience. I completely agree with you, it feels like a weird asymmetry that's very unhelpful. The focus on social and emotional development has been really challenging in the school system, because in the early-years setting it was agreed that we should focus on personal and social skills, and on children managing their relationships. But with older children, it's as if they don't need it. As if at the age of five you're fully formed and done – well, I'm not fully formed and done! I'm still developing in terms of personal and social skills, everybody is!

We can't say that up to a certain point social relationships are important, wellbeing is important or kindness is important and then, after that point, okay, now let's get down to the serious business, because we've got GCSEs to think about. That's where I feel we've lost something fundamental about being a human being and how we're all developing throughout our lifetimes. Of course it makes sense for us to keep prioritising kindness.

As this year of daily kind acts drew to a close, it was clear that I still had a lot to learn about kindness. And since then, there have been increasing amounts of studies, research and resources created to help us all understand its importance. The findings of The Kindness Test alone are a fascinating and encouraging read – you'll find the link to all the resources in the chapter notes at the end of the book: do check them out. I played a small part in the study as I was included in a short BBC Ideas

Journey's End

film called *The Woman Who Was Kind Every Day for a Year*, together with my friend and neighbour Mr Patel, Professor Banerjee and Nina Anderson, who in lockdown 2020 set up a letter-writing campaign to connect school pupils with older people.

Meanwhile, back in August 2012, I had just a couple weeks of my mission left. I took ice creams to the firefighters at our local station on a particularly hot day, gave a stranger in Hoxton a beautifully wrapped 'Happy Unbirthday' present, took some ring doughnuts to the Olympics volunteers in Greenwich Park and helped a nice man called Derek find his way after we got chatting and he told me he was lost. I also sponsored a few people, made some charity donations and posted a book of Mary Oliver poems as a gift.

On the 366th day of my project, I went back to the Post Office where it all began. Alongside my sister Kimberley, my nephew George and my friend Kirsty, I told the people behind the counter the whole long story and took them a cake. They were amazed.

On the way home I came across two boys bickering at Canada Water tube station, and I asked them what they were arguing about. They told me they were brothers and they'd been 'getting on each other's nerves'. I bought two packets of Magic Stars and told them they could have one each if they promised to make friends. They agreed.

After that I went home. I felt a strange mixture of euphoria, pride and . . . disappointment. It was over. Finished. I'd done it. Mission completed. I didn't have to do it anymore. I'd get some time back. I'd probably have a bit more money! So, now what?

I knew I wasn't the same person who gave 50p to the boy in the Post Office 366 days ago. I'd learned so much, I still had so much to process and I had found the thing that would enable me to do some good in the world. I'd worked out that I had some healing and forgiving to do and had started that process. I'd discovered a way of using social media for something positive by sharing my adventures and getting loads of support in return. I wanted to persuade everyone that to be kind and to notice kindness was life-transforming and had the potential to be world-changing.

So what to do now? How could I deliver that message to everyone? To carry on or not to carry on? Well, that was the question . . .

After
Starfish

I did carry on with my daily acts of kindness after that first year. I realised pretty much straight away that this was the best thing I had ever done. Even though I said at the beginning that 'maybe I could be the best at being kind', of course I quickly discovered that it wasn't about being the best, but about doing your best. I realised that if I did a kind thing every day, no matter if it was only small, if it was in the right spirit, to make someone's life, day, hour, minute a little better, well, that was enough. And I have done this now for more than a decade.

Once that first year was up, I celebrated at Woolfson and Tay gallery in Bermondsey with an exhibition of words and images designed by my friend Jessica Worrall. Friends visited from far and wide: my dear friend Cindy Parsons from the Isle of Wight came along, as well as Steve Richards, my pal from school who surprised me with a visit all the way from Thailand. Christine and Asif, who had helped me on Valentine's Day, were there, and many other friends popped in throughout the day. We had lots of tea and cake. Sharon Calcutt joined us and 'took the baton' from me, beginning her own year of kindness there and then. I'm delighted to report that many people have joined in since, for a week, a month or longer, trying out their own acts of kindness.

And I found myself thinking about my biological dad. I looked back at that year of kindness when he kept popping back into my head. I'd kept wondering if he'd heard me on the radio or seen me in a magazine and if he'd get in touch. He didn't.

Eventually, life intervened in the way it often does. I wrote two children's books about kindness, and when they were published was invited to write a piece about the 'Top 10 philosophical questions children should ask' in the *Guardian*. Then my half-brother's wife saw the article and left me a friendly message on Facebook. This gave me the impetus to ask our uncle for help in meeting up with my dad, and he was glad to do what he could. It was risky emotionally. He'd already rejected us twice. But they say, 'Third time's a charm', so I gave it a go. And so it was, with the knowledge and skills I had gained and with my sister-as-ally at my side, that on Friday 13 May 2016 I got packed and ready to travel to Belfast to see our father.

Natalie and I were due to meet him at a pub in Belfast city centre. It had been organised by our uncle and aunt, who had also very kindly paid for our flights. Our uncle had wanted it to be a surprise for Dad, but was thankfully persuaded by our aunt to tell him what was going on. It might have been a little intense as a surprise visit. I felt a bit apprehensive about the date, but I told myself that that was just a silly superstition, and it made me smile.

We waited. And we waited. He eventually turned up an hour and twenty minutes late, apparently because he 'had to have a lie in'. To be fair, our half-brother's wife had warned me that this might be the case, as he was always late.

When he finally arrived, he bought himself a drink and then talked non-stop about himself for an hour. He didn't ask either of us a single question about ourselves. But he did invite us to visit his house the next day.

His second wife had passed away and he lived alone. He seemed to find it hard to remember anything about our mum, but he was keen to be reassured that she was happy now. Later he took us out on his little boat, and afterwards we drank Styrofoam cups of tea, sitting on a bench outside the café, all in a row like three wise monkeys. I asked him why he didn't try to get in touch, and he said that he'd thought we were young enough to 'start again' and 'have a new dad'.

Starfish

I told him exactly what that 'new dad' had been like, and I didn't pull any punches. In the moment of telling him, I realised for the first time that I had always apportioned some of the blame of what had happened to us as children onto him, and that that was unfair, as he couldn't possibly have known. But surely he would have known that not keeping in touch with us would have made us sad, I thought. He said he hadn't as he 'didn't want to upset the children'. I responded, 'We are your children too.' I am proud that I was as honest as I could be in that moment.

That evening we all went to dinner in a jazz club. There was a live band. Dad sang along, he seemed to love it. It was as pleasant an evening as it could be in the strange circumstances. Over the next few days, my sister and I did all the tourist stuff, just the two of us. We toured the Peace Walls, drank Guinness and visited the *Titanic* Museum. We met one of our half-brothers and his wife, which was nice. It was a fun trip, in the end, thanks to them and to my sister, aunt and uncle.

Dad rang the day we were leaving and promised to visit when he came over to England. He seemed to mean it at the time. He never has visited. I found out a year later he had come over to London, but he hadn't rung.

For anyone who has been abandoned by a parent, for any reason, I think it's hard not to put them on a pedestal, even if you don't know that is what you are doing. It's common to idealise the one who is missing. I certainly did this. When I was at primary school, I had told the other kids that my real dad 'looked like Elvis' because that is what I really truly believed. I had one photo of him as a very young and handsome man, with me as a baby on his lap. For a long time, I expected him to come and rescue us from our stepfather, or to turn up with gifts of riches, or at least a castle. Real fairy-tale stuff. It's hard for a regular human being to live up to those expectations. But I tried to think of him kindly, even after that disappointing visit.

Conversations on Kindness

I considered everything I had learned about the kindness of forgiveness. I thought about how I didn't know my father's side of the story; or what he experienced serving in the British Army in Belfast in the 1970s at the height of the troubles, when rioting was common, bombings of public places by both loyalists and republicans increased, and both sides perpetuated violent, deadly atrocities. I couldn't imagine what he had seen or been through. He married a local woman, and his sons were born in Northern Ireland. But that's all I knew, a few bare facts. I have never lived through conflict; I have never seen violence on that scale. I can imagine that it would be hugely traumatising.

Maybe he was late to meet us that day because he was nervous; maybe he didn't ask us about ourselves for the same reason. Or maybe he was worried about the answers we might give him. And how could he live up to my fantasy of what he was anyway? Only Elvis can be Elvis, after all, and probably even the King disappointed his daughter sometimes. I had to find it in myself to have compassion for my dad, to accept he did his best, to forgive him for letting us down, me and my sister and my mum. And to accept that what happened afterwards had not been his fault.

It took a bit of work, forgiving him. I had to admit first how much his abandonment had hurt me, long into adulthood. So, finally, this year, I wrote to him.

I said that I understood that he had done his best and that neither of us knew what each other's lives were now or had been since we last saw each other. I wrote that my imagining him had got me through some dark times, and thinking he was probably desperately trying to find me was a comfort. I told him about all the things I had done to try to get his attention, trying to be famous because I thought that could only improve my chances of him wanting to know me. I told him that I forgave him for hurting me and my sister and that I didn't think he had meant to. That I wished him well, and all his family well too. That

Starfish

I was writing about him in my new book, and sharing the story of what had happened, so that he knew. It was a short letter, and simple, and a relief to write and post it. It did feel like a way of being kind to myself, and to him.

The theatre show Gareth and I went on to create to tell the story of the year of kindness, which toured from 2014 to 2016, was revived and simplified in 2020 so that it fit in a suitcase. I travelled about in the pockets of time we were allowed during the long Covid lockdowns, and told my story in pubs, village halls and libraries all over the UK. It was incredibly moving to be having conversations with people about kindness during this time, when there was so much isolation, loss and suffering, but so much community spirit and kindness too. I realised that this story still had enormous power and resonance for people.

And there was so much more to worry about now: the world felt more hazardous than ever. Terrible ongoing wars and conflict, human suffering and cruelty, injustice and corruption, climate change and the battle to save our planet: all these things felt overwhelming again, and I came back to the questions I had asked myself so long ago – what can I do to help? And is it enough, in the current circumstances, to be kind in these small ways?

There were two people I knew I needed to talk to, to help me find my way onwards. The first was Susie Hills, the founder of Teamkinduk, a community-interest company whose flagship annual online festival of kindness, KindFest, takes place around World Kindness Day on 13 November. Susie has such a great overview of the sort of thing that people are doing in connection with kindness, I knew that chatting with her would help clarify things for me.

What's the Kind Thing to Do?
with Susie Hills

Firstly, I want to thank you for creating KindFest, which I really appreciate being part of. It's helped people realise that there is an ecosystem of kindness out there, and it has created a place where we can all come together. Can you tell me how the idea came to you?

Well, my mum died a few years back, and lots of extraordinarily diverse people came to her funeral, who I had never ever met. They all said that my mum had been incredibly kind to them in different ways. That really resonated with me. So I bought every book I could find on every aspect of kindness, and I committed to giving a presentation at a conference on kindness and leadership. And because I committed to doing that, I had to do the work!

That's exactly what I did at the beginning of my journey too. Made a public declaration to keep me to it!

So I did loads of reading and created this presentation. Then I was thinking about all the people that I had come across, who had written books and done things about kindness, and I wondered if we could have a festival on kindness. So, we created KindFest, at the time when everybody needed something, during lockdown in 2020. We got some amazing speakers, who are all passionate about kindness. I know they do extraordinary things, and they're people that I would never have got to meet in my day-to-day work as well. So this incredibly uplifting community came out of it.

The theme of 'radical kindness', which you chose for 2023 KindFest, intrigued me, as it is a phrase I have been thinking about a lot. I wondered why you chose that theme, and what radical kindness is to you?

I felt if we focused on radical that we could be brave and talk about difficult things. There is a danger that kindness can be seen as fluffy, and there's nothing wrong with random acts of kindness. To give somebody flowers or leave a message for people – it's just a beautiful thing to do. But there's also kindness which deals with tough things, and that can take years. It's a type of kindness that must challenge, and it's difficult. So I was hoping that by using the theme radical kindness we could get some of those trickier discussions going. But we must be able to talk about difficult things with kindness, of course.

Yes, it feels important because we live in such divisive times, to stay in conversation with each other, to try to find common ground. What I've learned with difficult conversations is to not shame other people for their actions or standpoint, because if you do that it shuts down the dialogue. If you take shaming out of it, and you can say, 'I hear you, but maybe could consider this or that', then the conversation can continue. Which feels so important.

Yes, it's this idea that we must just cancel each other out if we disagree on something, and just shame and blame something or someone into oblivion.

And what that means is we don't feel we have permission to make a mistake, or to change our minds, or grow.

It's quite scary to say something out loud, because people pile in, you know. You think, *Can I say something and make a mistake? Is there something that I need to learn here?* Because maybe I need to learn to use different language, maybe it's inappropriate or makes someone else feel uncomfortable. But you hope that people will with kindness point something out to you that you need to learn. You know we need to be able to help each other to do better.

Yes, it requires courage to stay in a difficult place with someone and to learn from each other. I love the idea also of radical slowness in connection with being kind and I think you told me this was something you were interested in?

There was an interesting bit of research about the importance of slowing down. There were two groups of students, and one group was told they had to get to this lecture quickly and the other group were told not to rush. Both groups came across somebody who needed help because they'd collapsed. And none of the group who were told to be quick stopped to help the person, but the group that were told not to rush all stopped to help. The research concluded that if people are feeling like they must rush, their ability to be kind diminishes. So rushing about, which we are under pressure to do, is a big barrier to being kind.

If you are rushing, you're more likely to type an email that isn't very kind. You're more likely to snap at somebody or not notice that they just need some help. So I think one of the biggest things we could do is just slow down a bit, and we'd be much kinder because of it.

I wonder what other changes we would need to make in the world to help support kinder societies?

I'd like us to be able to know how to use kind language. To be able to talk about kindness and for that to be completely normal. And for people at a young age to be able to understand when something is kind or not kind and talk about it. So you can point out to somebody that what they've just done isn't very kind, and that would be a normal thing to say.

If you could give one message to everyone about kindness, what might that be?

I think I'd say, ask yourself the question, 'What's the kind thing to do?' often. I think that question opens a whole world of things that are beautiful. It's the question that I always ask when I'm stuck, and it never has failed to give me a good answer. When my son was poorly and he had mental health issues, I found it really challenging to know sometimes how to be with him. But that question never failed me, in knowing what to do to help him, that the kind thing to do was just to sit next to him. There's nothing I can say. There's nothing that I can magically do, but I can sit next to him. So, you know, whatever the situation was, that question has never let me down.

Talking with Susie and watching KindFest had helped a lot in my quest to find a way for myself moving forward.

The second person I knew I needed to speak to was one of my oldest friends, Gaylene Gould. We have known each other since university, when she appeared as if by magic one day as I was on the banks of the river telling stories. Gaylene seemed to me to have found a way to express herself creatively and be of service, in such beautiful ways; her work is deep, inspiring and quietly radical.

The Art of Kindness
with Gaylene Gould

I'd love to hear about the spaces that you create for people to come together, and how you came to focus on that, as it is something I long to do too.

Well, it came from thinking that if we learn how to relate to ourselves first in a much kinder way, a more curious way, then that would allow us to relate to others in a kind and curious way, and the world about us. I thought if I created spaces that allowed us to practice this then something beautiful might happen. It's great to focus on inviting people to care for themselves. It feels important.

A lot of your work is about healing.

Yes, I have been working on something called the Black Mary Project. In the seventeenth century, according to legend, a black woman called Mary Woolaston lived and worked on the Kings Cross/Clerkenwell border, and she was the keeper of a healing water well. So the project is an artistic imagining of a twenty-first-century healing well, and what that might look like for London today.

The pandemic meant we recently experienced so much loss, suffering and pain on a global scale. That compassionate part of people opened because of that collective experience. People began asking genuinely different questions like, what am I here for? What is my purpose? How do I sustain myself through all this up and downing? How do I feel cared for?

Art really has one job and that is to make us feel. It's the only career that has that in the job description. The reason why this is important to change-making is because when we begin to feel we begin to transform.

It allows us to build compassion and empathy for others and to explore ourselves in a more compassionate way and triggers our curiosity. If art achieves this then it has done its job well. Tony Benn, the MP, when he was asked, 'Which politicians are going to be remembered?', responded that it's the artists who will be remembered, the writers and the storytellers. If you think about it, he has a point.

We all know the stories that are left behind. They're the ones that give us a sense of not just what happened, but how to feel about what happened. It's important that we understand the power and importance of stories and feelings. I see lots of artists becoming direct activists, and the language of politics and activism being adopted more and more and, given the desperate state of the world, I understand why. I also think you are already an activist by making work that allows people to feel, that blows people's hearts and minds open!

Starfish

I was speaking with Susie Hills about radical kindness too, and I wondered what that looks like for you.

It makes me think of a scenario where somebody is in a position of power and because of their own blind spots that space is not functioning well, their behaviour is causing harm. Is it a kind thing to remove that person or is it kinder to appeal to them hoping they will change? Sometimes it's kinder to remove them, to say it's time for you to leave. Being brought up as a girl, and taught to be sweet and kind, that type of radical kindness I can find hard. So radical kindness can take great courage to speak a truth that might be overlooked, either willfully or out of a lack of awareness.

I have been thinking about how forgiveness, kindness, all that stuff, is expected more from some of us, particularly women.

Absolutely. I'm in the process of unlearning some of that, the desire to be kind and pleasing. It can dampen down a very important voice and truth.

At the beginning of my adventure, in the first year, I asked myself the question – can kindness change the world? And I would like to put that question to you.

Without a doubt. I should add that kindness, radical and otherwise, almost always changes the world for the better because there are other responses that change the world for the worse. For instance, war changes the world too. All our responses cause a ripple effect. Behaviour begats similar behaviour. It is not that violence as a way to repel oppressive forces is not sometimes necessary. It's just that, as a species, this has become our only transformational method. We have yet to test another approach to co-existence that centres mutual respect and care. If we start with kindness towards ourselves that often makes kindness towards others – a community, society, the whole planet – easier. We are less fearful, more attentive, more aware. Fundamentally, a courageous commitment to kindness is the only thing that's going to change the world for the better.

Is there anything you would suggest for people to do to help make the world a kinder place?

Yes, start by practicing with yourself; begin simply by talking to yourself kindly. If we all did that, I'd be curious to find out what the ripple effect might be.

More than a decade after my first year of kindness, I know that I still have both a lot to learn and a lot to unlearn. It took me a long time to accept that the darkness and the light can and do co-exist in all of us. Not in a binary way, but more in a mixed-up, 'it's complicated' kind of way. It was only when I accepted this that I gained anything like what you might describe as wisdom.

Moving forward, I would like to learn how to be a better coach to myself, rather than a harsh critic. To deepen self-compassion so I can be the best I can be, to show up as best I can in the world, to serve as best as I'm able. To know myself and my potential and limitations, and to accept them. To be an ally to those who need it or ask for it, to be more empathic, more compassionate, more loving, kinder. To speak my privileges aloud, to count my blessings, to practise gratitude because it helps more than anything. To share ideas, resources, advantages, food, space. To love this still beautiful world as hard and as vividly as I can, to try to be happy, because the world's suffering is not diminished by my misery. To share the immense beauty of the world with everyone.

Because I do love the world and sometimes it tears at my heart, this love, and it hurts because we humans are so awful sometimes, but also, we are so beautiful. To love the world fiercely is to go deeper into kindness.

Starfish

What I am aiming for in the future is to practise radical kindness. What this will look like, well, I'll find out. But for me, radical kindness is about action, and it expects and demands a change of all systems, a complete upheaval of the way the world is and what we are told to value. It is demanding and rowdy, and it's an evolution, not a revolution. It offers a solution to everything, but asks everything of us, too.

Radical kindness is both unconditional love and tough love. Radical kindness teaches us to say to ourselves and each other, 'I will still love you if you behave badly, and I will let you know you hurt me, yourself, others or the world. Because I love you, I will tell you that I think you could do so much better.' Radical kindness invites us to go to battle not with guns and knives and harsh words but with love. It includes finding courage to 'speak truth to power'. To step aside when it's time for someone else to have a turn to speak.

Imagine if we asked those on opposite benches in the House of Commons just to love each other. How would they do that? How would that affect policymaking, the quality of their lives, the nature of political debate? Imagine . . .

Radical kindness is also about how we treat all the other earthlings: all the animals, insects, birds, plants, trees, as well as the rivers, beaches, mountains. I think it's high time for us to extend the 'us' to include the more-than-human, as many indigenous peoples do, as our ancestors most probably did too. So we don't say, 'Nature is in decline' but 'We are in decline'; not 'Wildlife needs protecting' but 'We need protecting.' These are subtly radical changes. They require deep thought, a decolonisation of thinking and behaving, a decentring of ourselves as human beings, recognising that we are just one part of a complex and interconnected system; a learning, unlearning and relearning.

I want to claim kindness as the radical and world-changing, life-transforming practice that it can be. And I want to encourage you to be kind to yourself too, to cherish and love and look after yourself as an act of resistance to the messages we receive that tell us to work harder, produce more, consume more, be better; the messages that tell us we aren't enough. Kindness is indeed a superpower that we all possess.

Kindness is one of the things that will offer you certainty in uncertain times. Because facts change, theories are disproved and proved and disproved again, history gets revised. What is constant in an inconstant world? Kindness. When I get lost, I come back to kindness – the guiding principle of all decisions for how you treat yourself, others and the world.

All that most of us can hope to do throughout our lives is to try to make the patch of earth which we live on as good as it can be, to reach out to our neighbours near and far with kindness, as much as we're able. In this way, together we can change the world for the better. Which reminds me, I have one last story for you. It was first told to me by Pete Sainsbury, the vicar with whom I spoke about religion as we sat in his lounge in Birmingham. This story has stayed with me ever since, and I have told and retold it hundreds of times. I think it perfectly illustrates the power of small acts of kindness.

The Star Thrower, adapted from the original by Loren C. Eiseley

Once upon a time, there was a little girl walking on a beach. There had been a storm and there were hundreds of starfish washed up on the shore.

From far away, a man watched as the little girl walked a few steps and threw a starfish back into the water. Then she walked a few more steps and threw another starfish back into the water.

The man walked towards the little girl. When he was standing right in front of her, he said, 'What are you hoping to do? There are hundreds of starfish on this beach, how can you hope to make a difference?'

Starfish

> The little girl looked at the man. She bent down, picked up a starfish and threw it into the water. Then she looked at the man and said, 'Well, it made a difference to that one.'

My many teachers over the last ten years have deepened my knowledge and belief in the power of stories. And I have learned that kindness starts with being kind to yourself and that this should and can coexist with kindness to others and the whole wide and still beautiful world. I am human and therefore imperfect. This is real life and not a fairy tale, so it doesn't end with a happily ever after: I still make mistakes, get overwhelmed and tired, have to remind myself to be kind to myself too. Sometimes I still feel sad; sometimes the unkindness of the world floors me.

In July 2024 my lovely mum got married to a kind and gentle man who we are all very fond of. It was a small wedding with close friends and family, full of silly dances, funny speeches, great food and laughter. As I looked around the room at my family in this beautiful setting, with the sun setting over the twinkling water in the background, I considered how fortunate I was, to have an amazing and eccentric family, a loving partner and such a rich and adventurous life. I knew in that moment that I had done very well. That my life was perfect in its own way, with all its imperfections, and I was too, with all my bumps and bruises and scars. I had done the very best I could, and that was enough. Then we drank a final toast and I persuaded everyone to do the conga.

I decided soon after the wedding to make some pledges moving forward – to renew my vows, you might say. You'll know by now how much I like a list. So here it is. What I, from this day forward, pledge to do, in no particular order:

> To help to heal the world through joy by creating places where people can come together and share stories, songs, dancing, music, food and fun

Conversations on Kindness

To be kind to myself by getting enough rest, taking time for meditation and walking, spending time with family and friends

To slow down

To persevere with difficult conversations

To continue caring for and planting trees

To be a good neighbour

To recognise that everyone is a neighbour

To chalk poetry on pavements at every opportunity

To make sure my garden is wildlife- and pollinator-friendly

To share resources, ideas, contacts and privileges

To eat healthy, seasonal, locally grown plant-based food as much as possible

To walk or use public transport as much as possible

To practise gratitude

To be an ally to those who need or ask for my support by signing petitions, donating, protesting and amplifying lesser-heard and unheard voices

To pass on and share hope via positive news

To celebrate the world and all earthlings

To truly be kind to *all* kinds

To listen to the world with care, to respond to what the earth needs, to the warnings and offerings of the world

To offer my gifts as a storyteller and artist

To serve kindness and peace in the world

To return to love, whenever I find myself in a place of fear

To change these pledges if any of them become no longer helpful!

So what about you, my friend? Have I persuaded you of the power of kindness? And what do you pledge? How might you be kinder to yourself, your community and the world? Here's a final thought from *Benedictus* by the Irish author and philosopher John O'Donohue:

> *There is a kindness that dwells down deep in things; it presides everywhere, often in the places we least expect. The world can be harsh and negative; but if we remain generous and patient, kindness inevitably reveals itself.*

Chapter Notes

Before: London's Burning

If you or someone you know is affected by any of the subjects in this chapter, here are some organisations that can help:

Childline: www.childline.org.uk

National Association for People Abused in Childhood: www.napac.org.uk

Refuge's National Domestic Abuse Helpline (free and available 24/7): 0808 2000 247

Samaritans (if you need someone to talk to, any time day or night): www.samaritans.org.uk or call FREE 24/7 on 116 123

Rebecca Solnit, *The Faraway Nearby* (London: Granta, 2022)

The article about the 2003 march protesting against the Iraq war can be found here: https://www.theguardian.com/uk-news/2023/feb/11/slugs-iraq-war-london-protest-2003-legacy

George Amponsah (dir.), *The Hard Stop* (2015), Ga Films, a documentary about the aftermath of the death of Mark Duggan, written and produced by George Amponsah and Dionne Walker

'Reading the Riots: Investigating England's summer of disorder – full report', *Guardian* in partnership with the London School of Economics, 14 December 2011; https://www.theguardian.com/uk/interactive/2011/dec/14/reading-the-riots-investigating-england-s-summer-of-disorder-full-report

Lenny Henry and Marcus Ryder (eds), *Black British Lives Matter* (London: Faber and Faber, London, 2021) – a brilliant series of essays focusing on the Black British experience, written in response to the international outcry at George Floyd's death.

'A riot is the language of the unheard' is a quote from Martin Luther King Jr's 1967 speech 'The Other America', available to watch here: https://www.youtube.com/watch?v=dOWDtDUKz-U

Chapter Notes

More information about Dan Thompson, who initiated #riotcleanup, can be found here: https://mrdanthompson.wordpress.com

More information about the Peckham Peace Wall can be found here: https://www.londonremembers.com/memorials/peckham-peace-wall

1. August: Try a Little Kindness

Wendell Berry, *The Peace of Wild Things and Other Poems* (London: Penguin, 2018). You can read the poem at www.scottishpoetrylibrary.org.uk

Sarah Winman, *When God Was a Rabbit* (London: Headline, 2011)

For more about the work of Dr Gillian Sandstrom, go to: https://gilliansandstrom.com

2. September: Flower Power

Dr Samara Linton and Dr Rhianna Wolcott (eds), *The Colour of Madness* (London: Bluebird, 2022)

Find out more about The Flower Bank here: https://www.theflowerbank.org.uk

Kindness Can Help Save Lives can be found here: https://www.bbc.co.uk/news/av/uk-54239886

3. October: Be Kind to All Kinds

Shaun Monson (dir.), *Earthlings* (2005), Nation Earth, an animal-rights documentary narrated by Joaquin Phoenix, is available on YouTube: https://www.youtube.com/watch?v=8gqwpfEcBjI&rco=1

Compassion in World Farming can be found here: https://www.ciwf.org.uk

Philip Lymbery, *Sixty Harvests Left: How to Reach a Nature-Friendly Future* (London: Bloomsbury, 2022)

Find out more about Kingsclere Estates at: https://www.kingsclere-estates.co.uk

More about National Park City can be found at: https://www.nationalparkcity.org

Chapter Notes

4. November: Another Day in Paradise

Erin Morgenstern, *The Night Circus* (London: Vintage, 2016)

More about the work of Crisis can be found at: https://www.crisis.org.uk

More about 1625 Independent People is at: https://www.1625ip.co.uk

Action for Happiness can be found here: https://actionforhappiness.org

Lots of resources about the Science of Happiness can be found here: https://ggsc.berkeley.edu/what_we_do/event/the_science_of_happiness

The World Wellbeing Movement can be found here: https://worldwellbeingmovement.org

Richard Layard, *Can We be Happier?* (London: Pelican, 2020)

The reference to Tolstoy is from his parable 'Three Questions', published in the collection *What Men Live By*. It is out of print, but may be obtainable through https://uk.bookshop.org

5. December: I Gotta Have Faith

Find out more about The Feast here: https://thefeast.org.uk

Claudia Hammond, *The Keys to Kindness* (Edinburgh: Canongate, 2022)

6. January: Bad News Blues

Find out more about Gleb Tsipursky here: https://www.givingwhatwecan.org

The podcast *If You Don't Know* can be found on the BBC, Spotify and Apple Music.

People Fixing the World is available via the BBC World Service: https://www.bbc.co.uk/programmes/p04d42vf

Time for Kindness can be found here: https://timeforkindness.co.uk

7. February: What's Love Got to Do with It?

You can listen to the chat I had with Billy Bragg, Reverend Richard Cole, Sian Williams & Co here: https://www.bbc.co.uk/programmes/b01qkwg2

Chapter Notes

More about Billy Bragg at: https://www.billybragg.co.uk

Get involved in changing politics for good here: https://www.compassioninpolitics.com

8. March: People Ain't No Good

Cardboard Citizens are here: https://cardboardcitizens.org.uk

Find out more about the Restore project at: https://www.theforgivenessproject.com/online-training/

The Prison Reform Trust's work is here: https://prisonreformtrust.org.uk

Read more about Black Lives Matter within the Criminal Justice System at: https://howardleague.org/wp-content/uploads/2021/06/A-guide-for-antiracist-lawyers.pdf

A charity supporting women in prison: https://womeninprison.org.uk

9. April: Born To Run

David R. Hamilton, *Why Kindness Is Good for You* (London: Hay House UK, 2010)

Action for Happiness can be found here: https://actionforhappiness.org

Kindness UK is at: https://kindnessuk.com

Sunday Assembly is here: https://www.sundayassembly.org

10. May: Compliment Slips

For details of Claudia Hammond's *The Keys to Kindness*, see notes for Chapter 5 above.

Dr Kristin Neff's work around self-compassion can be explored here: https://self-compassion.org

The Museum of Happiness can be found at: https://www.museumofhappiness.org

Chapter Notes

11. June: Amazing Grace

Dr Sharon Blackie's work can be found here: https://sharonblackie.net

The Forgiveness Project is at: https://www.theforgivenessproject.com.

The F Word podcast can be found on Spotify and Apple, as well as via The Forgiveness Project website.

Marina Cantacuzino, *Forgiveness: An Exploration* (London: Simon & Schuster UK, 2022)

12. July: Journey's End

You can watch the Opening Ceremony to the London Olympics 2012 here: https://www.youtube.com/watch?v=4As0e4de-rI

Natasha Khamjani's work can be found at: http://www.natashakhamjani.com

You can listen to The Kindness Test podcast here: https://www.bbc.co.uk/programmes/m000z5hf.

More about The Kindness Test itself can be found at: https://www.sussex.ac.uk/research/centres/kindness/research/thekindnesstest

13. After: Starfish

Dr Sharon Blackie's Substack *The Art of Enchantment* can be found here: https://sharonblackie.substack.com

You can find out about the theatre show *366 Days of Kindness*, produced by Applause, here: https://applause.org.uk/shows/366-days-of-kindness/

My *Guardian* article about philosophy for children is at: https://www.theguardian.com/childrens-books-site/2016/feb/14/philosophical-questions-children-should-ask-bernadette-russell

Information about TeamKind UK and KindFest can be found here: https://www.teamkind.org.uk

Gaylene Gould's work can be found here: https://www.gaylenegould.com

John O'Donohue, *Benedictus – A Book of Blessings* (London: Bantam, 2007)

You can read the original story of the star thrower here: Loren Eiseley, 'The Star Thrower' in *The Unexpected Universe* (New York: Harcourt, Brace and World, 1968)

Further Reading

In addition to those books about kindness mentioned in the chapter notes, I would also like to recommend:

Bregman, Rutger, *Humankind: A Hopeful History* (London: Bloomsbury, 2020)

Marco, Debbi, *The Power of Kindness* (London: Summersdale, 2020)

Also, here are some sources of kind and positive news to start you off. There are loads more out there, so good hunting!

The Ragged Optimist by Dan Thompson: https://danthompsonstudio.substack.com/p/ragged-optimist

Smiley Movement: https://smileymovement.org

Reasons to be Cheerful: https://reasonstobecheerful.world

Happy Eco News: https://happyeconews.com

Rewilding Britain: https://www.rewildingbritain.org.uk

Species United: https://www.speciesunite.com

Greater Good Science Centre: https://ggsc.berkeley.edu

The Uplift by Becky Barnes: https://theuplift.substack.com

Good News Dog: on Instagram @goodnewsdog

Who's Who

Our author:

Bernadette Russell is a performance storyteller, playwright and author who places kindness, hope, nature connection and positive mental health at the centre of her life and work. Her work aims to increase compassion and kindness through the arts, particularly through storytelling. She has created projects for many venues, including the Royal Albert Hall, National Theatre, BFI, National Trust, Southbank Centre and Royal Festival Hall. She is one of the storytelling team at Butser Ancient Farm in Hampshire, holds regular outdoor storytelling events at The Albany, Deptford, and The Clearing in Lesnes Abbey Wood, both in Southeast London. She teaches creative writing classes in collaboration with Treadwell's Books in Central London.

She is associate artist of immersive theatre company Teatro Vivo and dance theatre company Folk Dance Remixed, who combine traditional and hip-hop dance and music. She also produces work with her own company, White Rabbit, which she co-runs with Gareth Brierley, and collaborates regularly with artist Sophie Austin.

She has planted trees all over London as a volunteer tree-planting supervisor with Trees for Cities and is a volunteer tree guardian as part of the Street Trees for Living campaign.

She is the author of five previous non-fiction books for adults and children which focus on the power of small acts of kindness. For her ongoing project '366 Days of Kindness' she was chosen as one of the Southbank Centre's 67 Changemakers in 2015, and in 2017 was one of the recipients of People United's 'Be Kind' neon signs in recognition of her work.

Who's Who

Her work promoting kindness was the subject of a BBC documentary called *The Woman Who Was Kind Every Day for a Year* and can be seen here: https://www.bbc.co.uk/ideas/videos/the-woman-who-was-kind-every-day-for-a-year/p0bt6c4j

Our contributors, in order of appearance:

Dr Gillian Sandstrom is a Senior Lecturer in the Psychology of Kindness at the University of Sussex, and the Director of the Sussex Centre for Research on Kindness. Her primary research is on minimal social interactions with acquaintances and strangers, and her work on the benefits and barriers of talking to strangers was inspired by a smile-and-wave relationship that she developed with a lady who worked at a hot-dog stand. She contributed to The Kindness Test, a project conducting research into kindness, conducted in partnership with the BBC.

Kamilah McInnis is a journalist, writer, musician and mental-health advocate. She is the lead writer for *The Upbeat*, a BBC News newsletter sharing uplifting news. She also presents a BBC radio show on Friday nights, and is the author of *Windrush Wonders: Tales of Travel and Triumph*, an inspiring children's book about the *Windrush* generation. Through her work, Kamilah champions kindness, culture and community across various platforms.

Philip Lymbery is Global Chief Executive of Compassion in World Farming International, the leading farm-animal welfare environmental organization operating in more than forty countries on six continents; it is responsible for achieving major bans on some of the cruellest farming practices and corporate engagement that has resulted in commitments giving more than three billion animals every year better lives. Philip is a dedicated animal advocate, naturalist, photographer, award-winning author and proud dad to rescue dog Bruce.

Who's Who

Navdeep Deol heads the board of the National Park City Foundation and London National Park City. He is also a founding member of a local community group, Heston Action Group (HAG). Navdeep has been active with local community groups in Hounslow and West London for over four years, initially through litter picking but now supporting street and tree champions to improve and care for the green environment around them and in a local community garden. Through his volunteering he has actively encouraged collaboration across the city and contributed to local policies on important issues such as protecting biodiversity, water and waste management, enhancing the urban landscape and linking people to nature.

Marcus Fagon has over a decade of experience in youth and community work, with a specialty in mental health. He currently works with the Bristol-based charity 1625 Independent People, where he supports young people at risk of homelessness and delivers trauma-informed training to colleagues. In addition, Marcus freelances as an oral storyteller and facilitator. He specialises in leading myth-based transformational Rites of Passage weekends for young men, fostering deep personal growth and connection.

Richard Layard is an economist who thinks there is more to happiness than just the economy. He was one of the first economists to work on subjective wellbeing and has had a huge influence on making psychological therapy more widely available in the NHS.

Pete Sainsbury is an Anglican (C of E) priest and musician in parish ministry in Wiltshire. Despite the English surname, Pete is Irish and had a musical upbringing in Dublin before moving to London at the age of twenty-one to get involved in the music industry as a keyboard player. He didn't get far in terms of touring and big names, but he had a lot of impoverished fun along the way and did some interesting auditions! He thinks that kindness is something that still needs to grow a lot within him — including in his fathering of three young-adult children, and in his work as a pastor and priest.

Sarah Browning is Chief Kindness Cheerleader at Time for Kindness, a wellbeing programme which she founded. She believes that there is lots of kindness in the world, we just don't talk about it enough yet. She founded the programme to inspire kindness and to teach others to notice it too.

Billy Bragg — the 'Bard from Barking' — is an English singer, songwriter, musician, author and political activist. His music blends elements of folk music, punk rock and protest songs, with lyrics that mostly span political or romantic themes. His activism is focused on positive social change and left-wing political causes.

Sandra Barefoot is the creative co-lead of The Forgiveness Project. She has over thirty years' experience of working in group facilitation, action research, project management, mentoring and creative programme development, with specialism in multi-disciplinary arts practices inclusive of theatre, dance, visual arts, poetry and sign language. Sandra works alongside storytellers to create online resources, and managed the development and facilitation of The Forgiveness Project's prison programme RESTORE. From this work, she identified that shame frequently lies at the root of what prevents us from healing and, as a joint research fellow of the Griffin Society of Cambridge University's Department of Criminology, she researched the place of shame and its impact on women's lived experiences. This investigation has led Sandra to collaborate with other organisations both in the UK and globally to develop a community of practice that centres on the

Who's Who

facilitation of spaces where our stories of shame can support personal and collective healing.

Dr Dan Campbell-Meiklejohn is a psychologist and neuroscientist at the University of Sussex. He is passionate about learning about human social motivations, including our motivations to empathize and be kind.

Victoria Johnson is the co-founder and Director of the Museum of Happiness (MOH), a not-for-profit social enterprise that shares the science and art of authentic happiness in creative and reflective ways. Vicky is a happiness teacher, facilitator and mentor who works with schools, universities, workplaces, the NHS and government officials. MOH's mission is to help people make friends with their mind, befriend difficult emotions and together co-create a happier, kinder and more peaceful world from within.

Marina Cantacuzino is an author and broadcaster who in 2004 founded The Forgiveness Project, a charity that works with real stories to help break cycles of harm and create a more compassionate world. The latest of her three books on the subject of forgiveness is *Forgiveness: An Exploration*.

Natasha Khamjani is a choreographer, host and education specialist who has worked on many ceremonies with mass-movement choreography teams, including all four ceremonies for the London Olympics, the Commonwealth Games, FA Cup Final, Roald Dahl's City of the Unexpected, the Queen's Jubilee and the Eurovision Song Contest, as well as many parades and outdoor festivals. She is Co-Artistic Director of Folk Dance Remixed, a ground-breaking company fusing folk and hip-hop dance and music that tours nationally each year, as well as co-running a theatre school in London called DNPA. Natasha is a passionate and sought-after education specialist working for organisations including the Southbank Centre, Mimbre, East London Dance, Garsington Opera, the Royal Opera House, English National Opera, Grange Festival, Into Opera, Royal Academy of Dance, the children's charity CHIVA, Millennium Performing Arts and Southwark Music Services, plus various schools and colleges.

Professor Robin Banerjee is Professor of Developmental Psychology and the inaugural Pro-Vice-Chancellor for Global and Civic Engagement at the University of Sussex. Formerly Head of the School of Psychology, his research focuses on the social and emotional development of young people, and he works closely with practitioners and policymakers in the areas of education and mental health. He founded the Sussex Centre for Research on Kindness, an interdisciplinary research centre focused on illuminating the nature of kindness and its impact on people and communities.

Susie Hills is a kindness spotter and the Kickstarter of TeamKind – an online community of people highlighting and celebrating kindness – and founder of KindFest, the world's first online festival of kindness, which has celebrated World Kindness Day since it began in 2020. In 2019 she was named as one of fifty 'Leading Lights in Kindness' in the *Financial Times*, and in 2023 she was given a Positive Leadership Award. Susie is regularly asked to present on kindness, having done so for organisations such as Oxford University, AUA and CASE Europe, a not-for-profit that champions education. She writes regularly on kindness on her LinkedIn page and for Halpin, where she is the Joint CEO and Co-Founder. Halpin is a management consultancy for universities, providing governance, strategy, people and fundraising services.

Who's Who

Gaylene Gould is an artist who unearths buried stories in places and people to help us connect more deeply. She creates artistic experiences and digital collages that transform the places where people live, work and play. Her latest project, the Black Mary Project, reimagines an ancient healing well run by a mysterious seventeenth-century Black woman wellkeeper. She is a writer and a broadcaster and host of *Serpentine* podcast.

Thanks

I have so many people to thank – I hope that this list is comprehensive but forgive me if you think you should be on here and you're not! Like any creative project, this book is a collaboration with the hundreds of people who have spoken to me, advised me, challenged me and helped me, and I am grateful to everyone.

Firstly, to those I love most in the world:

My mum and my sisters, Kimberley Trim and Natalie Russell, who taught me how to be kind. I am so lucky to have such a lovely family, which includes George, Josie, Christopher, Ian, Brandon, Portia, Graham, Amanda, Janet, Keith, Emma and of course my amazing partner Gareth, without whom none of this would be possible. Gareth, I hope you know that I couldn't have done any of this without your support and guidance, as well as the very healthy soups you kept making me. I love you and I thank you a million times. I owe you so much soup.

Special mention to Lola the Woof for much fun and rolling in grass – you are the best of dogs.

To Nicola, James, John, Maggie and Andy, who were kind enough to help me on this journey despite the fact that it may have been challenging for them.

To my brilliant agent Julie Churchill at A. M. Heath, who is very wise about words and tea, among many other things. Thanks for taking time for long conversations when I needed advice or to thrash something out.

To my editor and publisher Sarah Rigby, who is kind, funny, wise and patient: I am so grateful to you for giving me the chance to write this book. You always make me feel better about everything. This is but one of your special skills.

Thanks

To Celia: thanks so much for your excellent, intelligent and sensitive work on editing and making this book so much more powerful and make so much more sense. I really appreciate the gentleness and wisdom of your notes – and I hope by the time this book is in print we will have met in person!

Thanks to the whole team at Elliot and Thompson, the most generous and kind publishers, who I am so honoured and grateful to be working with. This includes Lorne Forsyth (chair), Marianne Thorndahl (operations manager), Pippa Crane (editorial director), Katie Bond (publisher), Amy Greaves (Head of Publicity and Marketing) and Eluned Gulbekian (Publishing Assistant).

Thanks to Claire Maxwell of Read Maxwell Communications for being a brilliant publicist and to Marie Doherty for the beautiful typesetting.

Thanks also to Heike Schüssler for the incredible cover design and to printmaker Amy Gillespie, whose beautiful and uplifting image is at the centre of the cover.

Special mention to Sally Hughes, an amazing bookstagrammer (@Salboreads) and friend, whose unfailing encouragement helped me find the courage to write this book.

Thanks also to my counsellor Ana Janmaat, for all the talks and guidance, to Charlie Tunmore (health and wellbeing coach) and the NHS health team at Waldron Health Centre, as well as neuropsychiatrist Dr Timothy Nicholson at King's College Hospital. I am very grateful to the NHS for all their care and kindness.

To all the named and unnamed people who accepted my acts of kindness that year, or who nominated people and supported me. In order of appearance: Penny Dreadful Theatre Company, including Mira Dovreni, Phillipe Spall, Dennis Herdman, Denise Kennedy, Mick Barnfather, Ross Mullan and Ian Street; the Patel family at Krishna News, Brett Willcox, Roxanna Kennedy, Ryan in Tesco, Michelle Olmo and Miranda Llewellyn,

Thanks

Sophie Donnelly, Billy and Hannah Wolf and all my friends in Stan's Cafe Theatre Company, Ed Currie, Natalie Goulder, Jack Trow, Isabel Shapiro, Vanessa and George Woolf Hoyle, Kit Taylor, David Duchin, Kate Kamil, Paul Arvidson, Donna Bakewell, Cindy Parsons, Phillippa Lawrence, Alex Alderton, Henry Bouquet, Daniel Lynch, Andy Rees, Donna Lowe, Liz Hawkins, Flic Everett, Mary Corbett, Dan Thompson, Beth Kerslake, Ian White Wood, Judy Barrington-Smuts, Sally Reeve Edwards, Lisa Higgins, Eve Lumpy, Flic Everett, Rebecca Tonge, Maggie Gordon-Walker, Claire Poley, Karen Poley, Harriet Kershaw, Dawn King, Rachel Bollen, everyone in Wet Picnic Theatre Company, including Matt Feerick, Judy Barrington Smuts, Charlotte Dubery, Graeme Coburn and Viktor Lukawski; Van Demal, Callum Uprichard, Edwin, Morgan Nichols, Louise Halvardson, Yvonne Thornton, Rebecca Cubbit, Tina Moran, Sophie Donnelly, Kate Bohdanowicz, Caroline Jowett, Stephan Slater, Matt at The Mayflower in Bermondsey, James Yarker, Wendy Dumper, Joe Grayling, Siobhain Furlong, Doly Garcia, Simon Edge, Marion Gold, Rebecca Tonge, Penny Harrison, Joanna Jones, Mernie Gilmore, Debbi Marco, Laura Milne, Laura Jackson, Simon Edge, Charlotte Civil-Sullivan, Jules Craig, Glenn Stevens, Angus and the 'Broken Biscuit Society', Charlie at Madam Jojo's, Heather Burton, Nick Boardman, Jamie, *Time Out*, James and Kai Dolan, Christine Entwistle and Asif Iqbal, Leo and Theresa, Bev Freer, Kevin Head and Kirsty, Katie Clifford, Marnie Summerfield Smith, Wayne Lucas, Steve Mayo, Helen Tamblyn, Cathy White, Alexi Duggins, Stewart Whoo, Denise Flower, Abby Butcher and her mum, For Books Sake, Sarah Ratherham, Patrick from Winchester Discovery Centre, Helen Medland and Tim Harrison from The Basement, Johanna, Bex Davey, Anna Madeleine, Rhian Brain, Abigail O'Neill, Violet Skinner, Ava Bonham Garter, Sara Butcher, Celine Hispiche, Paschale Straighton, Gill Lloyd, Chief Dawethi, Sam Scott Wood, Damon Shaw, Portia Smith, Nicola Blackwell, Victoria Melody, Tamsin McCahill, Joyce Jewell, 2012 marathon runners including Sarah

Thanks

Wheeler (as requested by Beverley Freer), Samenua (as requested by Gaylene Gould), Kirsty Housley, Karen Knowles (as requested by Damien Cooper), Julia Belyaven (as requested by Chris Trim) and Nick Hutchins (as requested by Kim Trim), plus supporters Ian Payton, Samantha Boyd, Gerald Kyd, Kirsty McTaggart, Joyce Jacca and Annie Calvery; Gemma Seltzer, Marlene Redmond, Annaliza Jennings, Katherine Hunter, Claire Squires, Chris Wright, Fiona at the Magic Garden, Katie Lundie Hills and her mum, Jana Lapel-Denis, Vivacity Bliss, Jane Richardson, Jess Pearce, Wendy Attwell, Lynne Chapman, all at Jacksons Lane Theatre, Albany Deptford and Birmingham Rep, especially Roxanna Silbert, Tessa Walker, Adrian Berry, Gavin Barlow and Raidene Carter; Leela Bunce, Ursula Dares, Jackie Downs, Derek from Greenwich.

To all my interviewees who so generously gave their time and wisdom: Dr Gillian Sandstrom, Kamilah McInnis, Philip Lymbery, Professor Lord Richard Layard, Marcus Fagon, Pete Sainsbury, Sarah Browning, Billy Bragg, Sandra Barefoot, Dr Dan Campbell-Meiklejohn, Vicky Johnson, Navdeep Deol, Marina Cantacuzino, Natasha Khamjani, Professor Robin Banerjee, Susie Hills and Gaylene Gould.

Also, thanks to the following people who spoke to me about faith: Bharti Patel, Navdeep Deol, Helena Goldwater, Asif Iqbal and Annie Calvery.

Thanks to Applause Rural Touring and the INN Crowd for supporting and producing the show *366 Days of Kindness*, and to all the venues and audiences who have shared their stories with me. Special mention to Gerry Daley, who came along and heard how I was sick in her hat and yet still forgave me.

Thanks to my oldest and massively cherished friends the 'Pompey Girls': Alis Reid, Nell Reid, Kate Baily and Natalie Russell, for reminding me I have always been eccentric.

Thanks also to Emma Waterford, Jack Trow, Jules Craig, Dennis Herdman, Sophie Austin, Charlie Folorunsho, Vera Chok, Mark

Thanks

Stevenson, Kas Darley, Corinna Ilschner, Moira Kerrane, Philippe Spall and Mira Dovreni, who have helped me during the writing of this book just by being my friends.

Thanks to the community of Deptford where so much of this happened, to my friends and neighbours. Deptford is forever!

Thanks to Deptford Park, Oxleas Woods, Russia Dock Woodlands, Southwark Park and all the green spaces, birds and wild earthlings which have kept me steady throughout this process.

Thanks to Anya, Pete, Mattie and Barney for a writing retreat in leafy Hampton. Thanks also to Sam, Gerald, Marcie, Zari and Bibi for a writing retreat in beautiful Broadstairs.

The final heartfelt thanks must go to the young man in the Post Office who accepted my small offer of kindness, which began this journey that changed my life for the better.